Network+™ Lab Manual

Tami Evanson

San Francisco • Paris • Düsseldorf • Soest • London

SYBEX

Associate Publisher: Neil Edde
Contracts and Licensing Manager: Kristine O'Callaghan
Acquisitions & Developmental Editor: Linda Lee
Editor: Raquel Baker
Technical Editor: Robert Gradante
Book Designer: Bill Gibson
Graphic Illustrator: Tony Jonick
Desktop Publisher: Rhonda Ries
Project Team Leaders: Lisa Reardon, Leslie Higbee
Proofreader: Publication Services
Cover Designer: Archer Design
Cover Photographer: FPG International

ISBN: 0-7821-2641-3

Manufactured in the United States of America

10 9 8 7 6 5 4 3 2

Dedication

To Jason and Alex.

Acknowledgments

I want to thank the many people at Sybex whose combined efforts made this book possible: Education Sales Coordinator Lucia Capron, Associate Publisher Neil Edde, Developmental Editor Linda Lee, Editor Raquel Baker, Technical Editor Bob Gradante, Project Team Leaders Lisa Reardon and Leslie Higbee, and Desktop Publisher Rhonda Ries.

Table of Contents

How to Use This Book

This lab manual is a companion workbook to use with the *Network+ Study Guide* by David Groth, which is designed to prepare candidates for the Network+ Certification Test. This lab manual increases understanding of the concepts and procedures introduced in the text by providing hands-on experience. It also provides practical experience that will be invaluable in the networking field. To get the most from the labs in this manual, read through each carefully before beginning the Procedure section. Also, read the suggested reading referenced at the beginning of each lab. The reading will introduce and explain the concept that the lab focuses on. Before beginning the suggested reading or the lab procedures, read the Lab Report at the end of each lab. This will help you know what information to focus on in the reading and exercises.

Each lab is set up in an easy-to-follow pattern. Every lab provides the following:

- Objectives to be accomplished
- Suggested background material to read in the *Network+ Study Guide*
- A list of necessary hardware
- A list of necessary software
- An introduction to the material covered in the lab
- Step-by-step instructions to complete the lab
- A lab report to emphasize the important points covered in the lab

There are 30 hands-on labs that practice the major concepts introduced in the *Network+ Study Guide*. The labs are broken into sections and are complete with step-by-step instructions on how to accomplish the objectives. Some labs are completed at the Windows 95 workstation, while others require hands-on contact with the servers in the classroom.

Labs 1, 2, 8, 11, 12, 14, 24, and 29 introduce information that does not refer to a specific operating system. There are a few that require only paper and a good understanding of the material, while others will investigate and set up non-vendor–specific information on the workstation. Labs 3, 4, 7, 17, 20, 22, 23, 25, 27, and 28 are Novell-specific labs that investigate and troubleshoot issues directly related to the NetWare operating system. Labs 5, 10, 13, 15, 16, 18, 19, 21, and 26 relate to Microsoft products, primarily the Windows NT network environment. We will also look at some DOS utilities that are helpful in understanding the intricate details of a network.

Required Equipment

A 486, or newer, Windows 95 computer with at least 32MB of RAM is required. Workstations will need an external modem and a network interface card, with the appropriate software driver on a 3.5" floppy disk. You will also need a computer with the Linux operating system installed.

Two classroom servers are required for this lab: a Microsoft Windows NT Server and a NetWare 5 Server. Each student needs an administrative account on each server.

Support Equipment

- Serial mouse
- 3.5" floppy drive
- A network interface card
- Network connection with Internet connectivity
- A tape backup device attached to, and configured on, the NetWare 5 Server
- Access to a DNS server
- Three 3.5" floppy disks
- An external modem with cables

Required Software

- Windows 95
- Windows NT Server
- NetWare 5 Server
- Linux operating system installed on a computer
- Software drivers for the network interface card and the external modem

Required Tools and Supplies

- Anti-static wrist strap
- Anti-static mat
- Phillips screwdriver

Lab 1: Recognize the Physical Topology of a Network

Objectives

Upon completion of this lab, you will be able to:

1. Recognize the cable type of a network.
2. Recognize the physical topology of a network.
3. Understand the logical topology of a network.

Suggested Reading

Chapter 1 and Chapter 2, pages 43–46 and 51–52, *Network+ Study Guide*, David Groth, Sybex.

Hardware Needed

A functional network with at least one Windows 95 workstation.

Software Needed

None.

Introduction

To become a successful network administrator, you must understand the flow of data in a network. How data is transmitted through the network is determined in part by the following: the physical layout of the cable, the logical flow of data in the network, and the media type used to cable the network.

The most common type of cabling used in LANs is Category 5, or Cat 5, twisted-pair cable. This is easily recognized by the RJ-45 connector type on the card. The RJ-45 connector resembles a telephone connector (see Figure 1.1). You may also see a BNC connection, commonly used in 10Base2 (Thinnet) networks (see Figure 1.2).

This lab introduces you to the components that determine the topology of your network. The most common physical network topologies are ring, star, bus, and mesh.

FIGURE 1.1 An RJ-45 connector

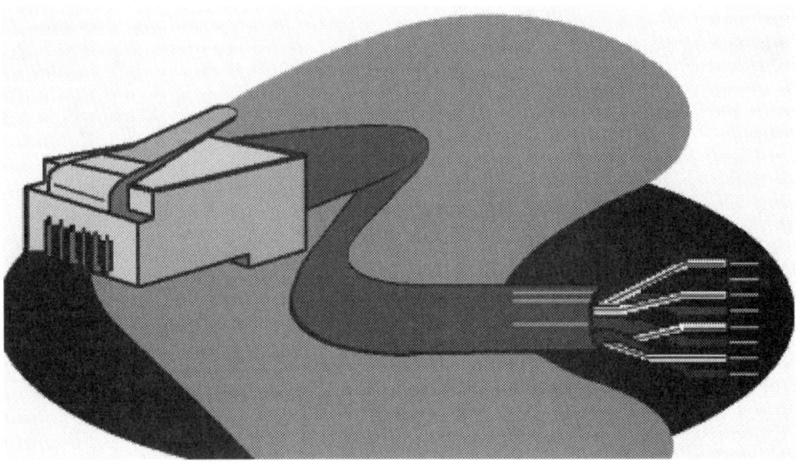

FIGURE 1.2 A BNC connector

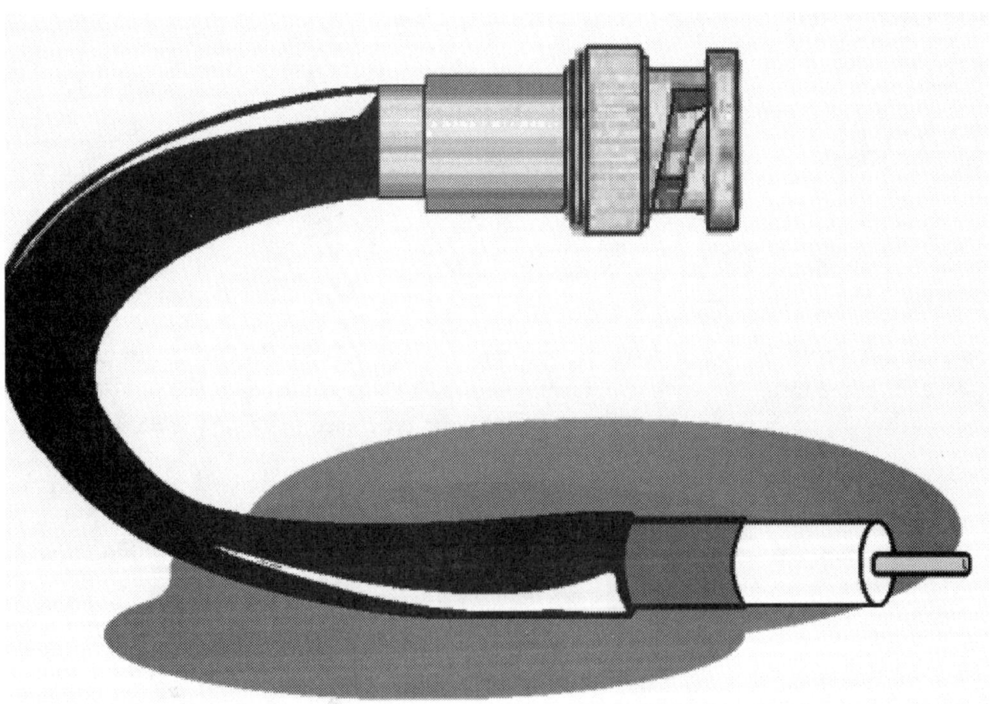

PROCEDURE

To Determine the Type of Network Interface Card in the Workstation

1. Turn on the workstation. The workstation will boot up to the Windows 95 Desktop.
2. Open the Control Panel utility by following this sequence:

    Start ➢ Settings ➢ Control Panel

3. In the Control Panel, select Network. You will see the network card installed in the workstation in the upper panel of the Configuration tab. This tab allows you to see the type of card installed. This information will give you the data needed to determine the speed of the network; and, often, the network topology.

To Determine the Type of Cabling Used in the Network

1. Position the workstation so you can see the back panel of the computer. You should clearly see the network interface card. The type of connector on the card will determine the type of cabling that is used on the network.
2. To prepare for the next exercise, follow the cable to its destination. Identify whether the cable plugs into a jack in the wall, into a hub, or into some other cabling connector.

To Determine the Physical Topology of the Network

1. First, you need to know the cable type (see the previous exercise). The next step is to investigate the physical layout of the cable. If there is a physical map of the network, this step is complete. If not, investigate the cabling structure in the network.
2. Identify the cable's destination from the workstation. If the cable goes into a wall jack, find the destination from that point. Does the cable extend to a patch panel, or does the cable go directly into a hub in the classroom? The cable may also extend to the next workstation in the network.
3. Draw a physical map of the network. The physical layout of the cable indicates the physical topology.

To Determine the Logical Topology of the Network

1. The physical topology of the network together with the cable specifications determine how the data flows through the network. Based on the information obtained in the previous exercise of the lab, determine if the logical topology is bus, mesh, star, or ring.

LAB 1: LAB REPORT

DATE ____________________ NAME ____

1. What are the specifications of the cable type used in the network you analyzed?

2. What is the physical topology implemented in this network? What are the advantages and disadvantages of the network's physical topology?

3. What are the specifications of the physical topology implemented in the network? What is the maximum segment length? How many segments/repeaters are allowed in this type of network?

4. Based on the information obtained in the lab, what is the logical topology of the network?

Lab 2: Identify the IP Address of a Workstation and the Class of the Address

Objectives

Upon completion of this lab, you will be able to:

1. Find and edit the IP address of a workstation.
2. Determine the class of a workstation's IP address.
3. Determine the gateway that is used by the workstation.

Suggested Reading

Chapter 4, pages 136–140, *Network+ Study Guide*, David Groth, Sybex.

Hardware Needed

A functional PC with Windows 95/98 and a TCP/IP protocol component installed.

Software Needed

None.

Introduction

The Internet's introduction to the public has made it necessary for network administrators to understand its language. TCP/IP is the language, or protocol, of the Internet. To communicate with the Internet, your organization's network must use the TCP/IP protocol suite. In the TCP/IP protocol suite, IP addressing is used to route information. This lab will introduce you to the fundamentals of IP addressing in a network.

PROCEDURE

To Find the IP Address of a Workstation

1. Turn on the workstation. The workstation will boot to the Windows 95 Desktop.
2. To open a DOS window, follow this sequence:

   Start ➢ Programs ➢ MS-DOS Prompt

3. Type **WINIPCFG**. This will give you the workstation's IP information (see Figure 2.1).

FIGURE 2.1 The IP Configuration window

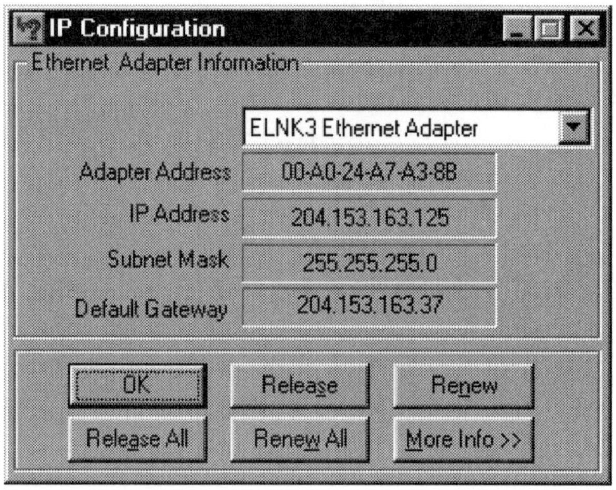

4. To edit the information, you need to access the TCP/IP protocol information in the Control Panel. To access the Network Control Panel, select the following sequence:

   Start ➢ Settings ➢ Control Panel ➢ Network

5. The Network window will appear. In the Installed Components field, find the TCP/IP component installed on your workstation. Click the menu selections once with the left mouse button. Next, click the Properties button.
6. The first screen displays the IP Address tab. This window shows the IP address and subnet mask for the workstation. Write down this information.
7. You may find the IP Address field dimmed. If the Obtain An IP Address Automatically radio button is checked, the workstation will contact the DHCP server for a temporary IP address (see Figure 2.2). For this exercise, we are using static IP addresses. To set up an IP address for the workstation, check the IP Address field. Enter an IP address configured for your network and with the subnet mask for your network.

FIGURE 2.2 The TCP/IP Properties window

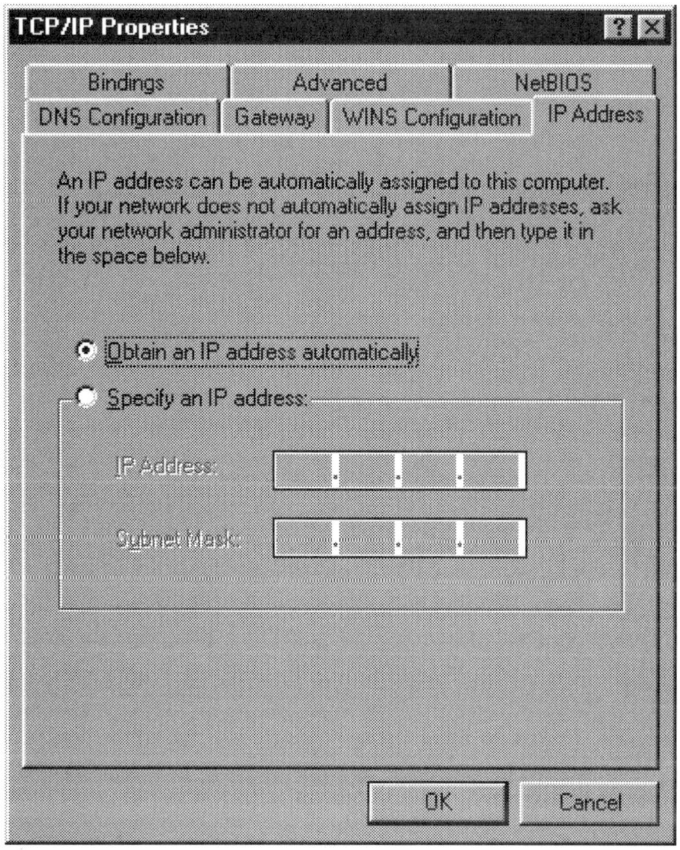

8. Click the Gateway tab. Write down the information displayed in the Installed Gateways field. If you are using DHCP in your network, you will not see a gateway entered.

LAB 2: LAB REPORT

DATE ____________________ NAME ____

1. Why is it important to configure IP addressing on a network?

2. What is the IP address and the subnet mask of the workstation that you examined in this exercise?

3. What is the class of the IP address configured on your workstation? How did you determine this?

4. What is a gateway? What gateway is configured on your network?

Lab 3: Install NetWare Client32 Software

Objectives

Upon completion of this lab, you will be able to:

1. Install NetWare client software from the CD-ROM.
2. Install NetWare client software across the network.

Suggested Reading

Chapter 3, pages 82–96, and Chapter 8, pages 292–293, *Network+ Study Guide*, David Groth, Sybex.

Hardware Needed

1. A functional, network-ready workstation with the Windows 95 operating system installed (minimum 486 with 32MB of RAM) and a valid network connection.
2. A working CD-ROM drive (if installing the client software from a CD-ROM).
3. The client software installed on the DATA volume of the server (if installing the client software from the network).

Software Needed

A NetWare Client32 installation CD-ROM.

Introduction

A workstation must be able to talk to the network. The workstation can talk to and use the tools available on a NetWare network by using the NetWare client. The NetWare client can be installed on a variety of workstation operating systems. For this lab, you will use the Windows 95 platform.

The NetWare Client 32 software is used widely because of the features it provides when logging into a NetWare network. It allows the client software to fully use Windows' features, including integrating into the Network Neighborhood and using the System Tray. The client software also gives the administrator the ability to edit, manage, and eliminate login scripts at the client level. The administrator has full control over the views in the client, so users can't edit their own settings.

You can install the NetWare client software in two different ways. If you are installing a small number of workstations, or if your workstation has no network connectivity, you should install the client software from the installation CD-ROM. If you are installing a large number of workstations, a better method is to copy the installation files to a central location on the network and install the client software from there. This lab will explain both installation methods.

When installing the NetWare client, you can choose from two different installation options: *Custom* or *Typical*. A Custom installation allows you to view the options available in the installation process. A Typical installation will automatically install and configure the default settings. Inexperienced users should install using this method. In this lab, you will use both installation options.

PROCEDURE

To Install the Client from the Installation CD-ROM

1. Turn on the workstation. The PC will boot to the Windows 95 Desktop.
2. Verify that you have a valid network connection by opening Network Neighborhood from your Windows 95 Desktop. If there is a valid network connection, you will see the network(s) listed in the window. Close the window.
3. Insert the CD-ROM into the drive. The NetWare Client Setup utility will automatically launch. The setup utility walks you through a series of settings before installing the software onto the workstation.
4. Choose English from the Language Setting screen.
5. The next option screen allows you to choose which software to install. For this lab, select the Windows 95/98 Client software installation (see Figure 3.1).

FIGURE 3.1 Installing the Windows 95/98 Client software

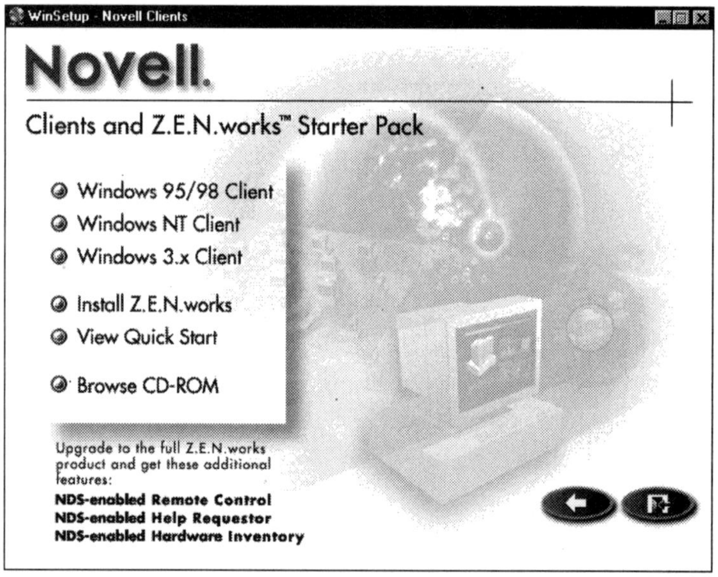

6. After selecting the client software to install, the licensing agreement appears. Read the text and select Yes to accept the licensing regulations.
7. The Welcome dialog box will appear. In the Select An Installation Option field, select Custom.
8. At the bottom of the window, click the Install button. The client software will be copied to the workstation. The installation may take a couple of minutes to complete.

9. After the client files are copied from the CD-ROM, reboot the workstation. During the reboot, the workstation displays messages to update the driver and software information. The workstation boots to the NetWare client Login screen.
10. In the lower-right corner of the screen, click the Advanced button.
11. Set the Tree, Context, and Server fields to the appropriate login location.

To Install NetWare Client Software from the Network

1. The instructor will create a file on the server called SETUP.EXE. (For this lab, the client software is already installed on the DATA volume of the server.) The instructor will copy the necessary installation files from the CD-ROM to the SETUP.EXE file and will give each user the appropriate rights. The user will need File Scan and Read rights to the directory holding the installation software.
2. Go to the SETUP.EXE installation file. To find the file, open Network Neighborhood. Double-click the Novell server displayed in the window. Double-click the DATA volume. Continue through the file system until you have located the appropriate file. (Your instructor will give you the path to the installation files.)
3. Select the SETUP.EXE file to install the NetWare client software onto the workstation. The client software's Installation utility will appear.
4. From first selection screen, select the language English.
5. Select the Windows 95/98 Client software installation.
6. The next screen allows you to look at documentation or begin the Novell client installation. Choose the Install Novell Client option.
7. Read the licensing agreement. Select Yes to accept it.
8. In the screen that appears, select the Typical installation option.
9. In the lower-right corner of the window, click the Install button. The client files will be copied to the workstation. This may take a few minutes.
10. After copying the files to the workstation, reboot the system. The PC will reboot and display the NetWare Client Login screen.
11. In the lower-right corner of the window, click the Advanced button.
12. Set the Tree, Context, and Server fields to the appropriate settings for the user.

LAB 3: LAB REPORT

DATE ____________________ NAME ____

1. For which workstation operating systems does Novell provide client software?

2. When would you install NetWare client software from the network instead of from the CD-ROM?

3. If you need to install 100 workstations with the Novell client software, what is the most appropriate installation method? Why?

4. What is the difference between a Custom and a Typical client installation?

Lab 4: Using NetWare Administrator to Add a User Object

Objectives

Upon completion of this lab, you will be able to:

1. Create a user object with NetWare Administrator.
2. Identify the different ways to create an object in NetWare Administrator.
3. Navigate in NetWare Administrator.

Suggested Reading

Chapter 3, pages 82–96, and Chapter 8, pages 319–327, *Network+ Study Guide,* David Groth, Sybex.

Hardware Needed

1. A working PC with Windows 95 installed.
2. An operational network running a NetWare 5 Server.

Software Needed

NetWare Administrator software.

Introduction

The basic tool used by network administrators of NetWare 5 networks is NetWare Administrator. This utility allows the administrator to control the NDS tree in one program. The functions available through NetWare Administrator include the following:

- Create and delete NDS objects and containers.
- Access the properties associated with objects and containers.
- Extend the NDS schema to allow for the administration of add-on programs that are installed on the NetWare 5 Server.
- Control security.

This lab focuses on the administration of user accounts, which is a vital function of NetWare Administrator. The exercises will familiarize you with the NetWare Administrator environment and give you a foundation upon which to build your knowledge.

PROCEDURE

To Launch NetWare Administrator

1. Turn on the workstation. The PC will boot to the Windows 95 Desktop.
2. Open Network Neighborhood. Find your NetWare 5 Server.
3. Double-click your server and find the SYS: volume.
4. NetWare Administrator is in SYS:PUBLIC\WIN32\NWADMN32. Launch NetWare Administrator.

To Create a User Object in NetWare Administrator

1. Click the container you want the object to be created in.
2. To create an object in a container, you can do one of the following:
   - Right-click the container object and choose Create from the pop-up menu.
   - Press the Insert key.
   - Choose Create from the File menu on the menu bar.
   - Click the Create User button on the toolbar.
3. In the Choice window, scroll down to the USER object.
4. Highlight the USER object and click OK. The next screen will appear.
5. In the Login Name field, enter the login name that you'll assign the user. In the Last Name field, enter the user's last name. You can also configure optional fields, such as Use Template, Create Home Directory, and Create Another User.

> **NOTE** It is essential to enter the user's login name and the user's last name when creating a user object in NetWare Administrator. There are other options that you can specify, but only the Login Name and Last Name fields are required.

6. Select the Define Additional Properties check box and click OK. The USER object's Indentification Property page will open.

7. Define the additional options for the user as appropriate (see Figure 4.1):

    Login Restrictions Restricts login options, such as the number of concurrent logins to the network and the login location based on the hardware address.

    Password Restrictions Restricts password options, such as the password's length and expiration date.

    Login Time Restrictions Sets a time limit on access to the network based on the time of day.

    Network Address Restrictions Limits a user's network access to only one workstation.

    Login Script Customizes the user's environment by creating a user login script.

    Intruder Lockout Provides a security feature to avoid network intrusion.

    Rights To Files And Directories Sets the security parameters for accessing various files.

    Group Memberships Allows administrators to create groups to manage users.

    Security Equal To Provides a temporary resolution to network access issues.

    Postal Address Contains a user's personal address information.

    Account Balance Limits the user's access time.

FIGURE 4.1 Entering additional properties for the user

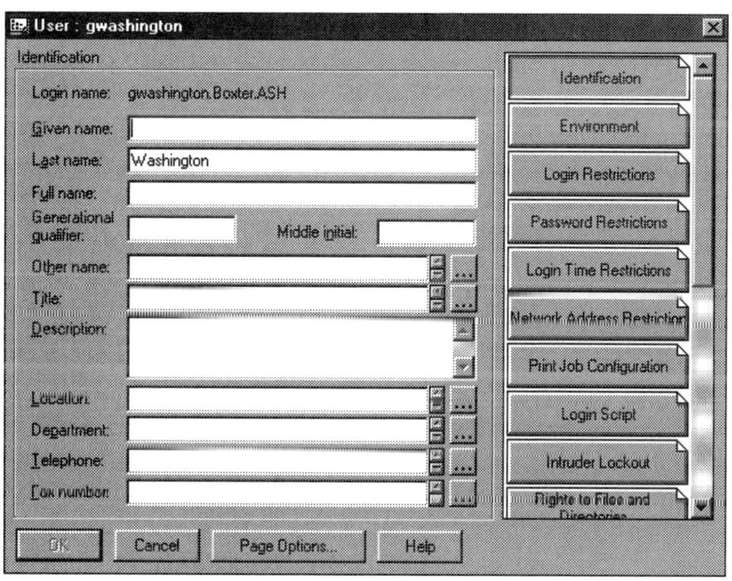

8. After completing the user information, click OK.

9. You can view the user information by right-clicking the USER object and choosing Details.

LAB 4: LAB REPORT

DATE ____________________ NAME ____

1. What are the three ways to create an object in NetWare Administrator?

____

____

____

____

2. What are the required fields for creating a user object in NDS?

____

____

____

____

3. Explain the purpose of creating login restrictions for a NetWare user.

____

____

____

____

4. What is the purpose of a user login script? When would you use a user login script?

____

____

____

____

Lab 5: Use User Manager for Domains to Create, Delete, and Rename a User in Windows NT

Objectives

Upon completion of this lab, you will be able to:

1. Create a user in User Manager for Domains.
2. Delete a user in User Manager for Domains.
3. Rename a user in User Manager for Domains.
4. Navigate in User Manager for Domains.

Suggested Reading

Chapter 3, pages 106–108, and Chapter 8, pages 307–311, *Network+ Study Guide*, David Groth, Sybex.

Hardware Needed

An operational Windows 95 workstation attached to a Windows NT network.

Software Needed

User Manager for Domains installed on the Windows 95 workstation.

Introduction

The fundamental tasks of a network administrator are creating and managing user accounts. The user account allows the network administrator to set security and determine access to network resources. Network resources can be managed from a central location with the User Manager for Domains.

The exercises in this lab demonstrate the daily account management duties that you will have as an administrator. To modify account information using User Manager for Domains, you must be logged into the domain with administrative privileges. Adding a user account is necessary for new employees, upon transfer of employees to different locations, and when adding employees who need access to network resources. You will need to delete an account if a user transfers out of the area or leaves the company. You will need to rename an account when a user gets married or changes his name. You may also opt to change the name on an account when you want to transfer a former employee's duties to a new employee taking over the same job responsibilities.

PROCEDURE

To Create a User in User Manager for Domains

1. On the Windows 95 workstation, use the following sequence to launch User Manager for Domains:

   Start ➢ Programs ➢ Administrative Tools ➢ User Manager for Domains

2. Click the User menu once. Select the New User option from this menu. This launches the New User dialog box.
3. Enter the user's name in the text box.

   NOTE It is essential to enter a user name when creating a user account through User Manager for Domains. There are other options that you can specify, but the only required field is for the user's name.

4. Complete the remaining optional fields as desired. These fields include:
   - Full Name
   - Description
   - Password (and Confirm Password)
   - Groups (user belongs to)
   - Hours (available for login)
   - Account Disabled
   - Password Never Expires
   - User Cannot Change Password
   - User Must Change Password at Next Login
5. In the upper-right corner of the New User window, click the Add button.

To Delete a User in User Manager for Domains

1. On the Windows 95 workstation, use the following sequence to launch User Manager for Domains:

   Start ➢ Programs ➢ Administrative Tools ➢ User Manager for Domains

2. Click the user you want to delete.
3. Go to the User menu.

4. Choose the Delete option.

NOTE You will get a warning message each time that you try to delete an account from User Manager for Domains. Click OK to delete the account. If you select Cancel, the account will not be deleted.

5. Click OK to delete the user account.

To Rename a User Account in User Manager for Domains

1. On the Windows 95 workstation, use the following sequence to launch User Manager for Domains:

   Start ➢ Programs ➢ Administrative Tools ➢ User Manager for Domains

2. Highlight the user that you want to rename by clicking it once.
3. In the User menu, select Rename.
4. Type the new name in the dialog box.
5. Click OK.

LAB 5: LAB REPORT

DATE ____________________ NAME ____

1. Name five properties that you can configure for a user account.

2. List three situations in which you would need to rename a user account.

3. What options can you configure in the User menu?

4. What is the essential step when creating a user in User Manager for Domains?

Lab 6: Create, Edit, and Delete a Linux User Account

Objectives

Upon completion of this lab, you will be able to:

1. Create a Linux user account in two different ways.
2. Be familiar with Linux editing utilities.
3. Delete a Linux user account.

Suggested Reading

Chapter 3, pages 109–110, and Chapter 8, pages 334–348, *Network+ Study Guide*, David Groth, Sybex.

Hardware Needed

A working computer with the Linux operating system installed.

Software Needed

None.

Introduction

The Linux operating system is a recently developed freeware based on the Unix operating system. Quite a rage surrounds Linux systems because of the following:

- It can be customized to accommodate personal preferences.
- The open code allows you to do all the customizations on your own.
- It's free!

Because of its popularity, you should be familiar with the Linux operating system. In this lab, you will look at some of the Linux administrative tasks. You will also learn to add a user using two available command sets, edit some user account parameters, and delete a user account.

PROCEDURE

To Add a User Account with the adduser Command

1. Turn on the computer at the Linux workstation. The computer will boot to the command prompt.
2. At the prompt, type the following command:

   adduser [*username*]

   NOTE The adduser command will add the login name, add the home directory in the /HOME/USERNAME directory, and create a mailbox.

   The user account is now added to the system.

To Add a User Account with the useradd Command

1. At the Linux workstation, go to the command prompt screen.
2. At the command prompt, type the following command:

   useradd –m [*username*]

   NOTE When you add the –m option to the command, the system will create the home directory automatically.

To Change the Login Name

1. At the Linux workstation, go to the command prompt screen.
2. At the command prompt, type the following command:

   usermod –l [*new login name*] [*current login name*]

   The login name is now changed on the system.

To Delete a User

1. At the Linux workstation, go to the command prompt screen.
2. At the command prompt, type the following command:

   userdel [*username*]

   The user account is now deleted from the system.

LAB 6: LAB REPORT

DATE ____________________ NAME ________________________________

1. List three advantages of the Linux operating system.

____

____

____

____

2. What are the two commands used to add a user account?

____

____

____

____

3. What command allows you to modify the user account?

____

____

____

____

4. What command do you use to delete a user?

____

____

____

____

Lab 7: Use the ConsoleOne Utility to Create a Group in NetWare 5

Objectives

Upon completion of this lab, you will be able to:

1. Create a group using the new NetWare 5 utility, ConsoleOne.
2. Identify the features and functions of the ConsoleOne utility.

Suggested Reading

Chapter 3, pages 82–83, *Network+ Study Guide*, David Groth, Sybex.

Hardware Needed

A working NetWare 5 Server with StartX loaded.

Software Needed

None.

Introduction

There are several new features available in a NetWare 5 network. One such utility is ConsoleOne, a Java-based administrator GUI (graphical user interface) that allows limited administration to NDS. ConsoleOne can be used either at the workstation or the server console. In this lab, you will use ConsoleOne at the server.

This lab will introduce you to the ConsoleOne utility and how to navigate this program. Using ConsoleOne, you can create a user, a group, an organization, and an organizational unit object in NDS. The ConsoleOne screen does not give you the same capabilities available in NetWare Administrator. The only screens available are General Information, Members, and NDS rights.These are the only functions available through this utility, in NetWare 5. To access all of the NDS objects, use NetWare Administrator.

PROCEDURE

To Launch ConsoleOne from the Server Console

1. At the NetWare 5 Server console, enter the following:

   STARTX

   The GUI interface, which resembles Xwindows, appears.

2. Use the following sequence to launch ConsoleOne:

   Novell ➢ ConsoleOne

3. The ConsoleOne window launches (see Figure 7.1). Be patient; this is a Java utility, and it may take some time to launch the window.

FIGURE 7.1 ConsoleOne window

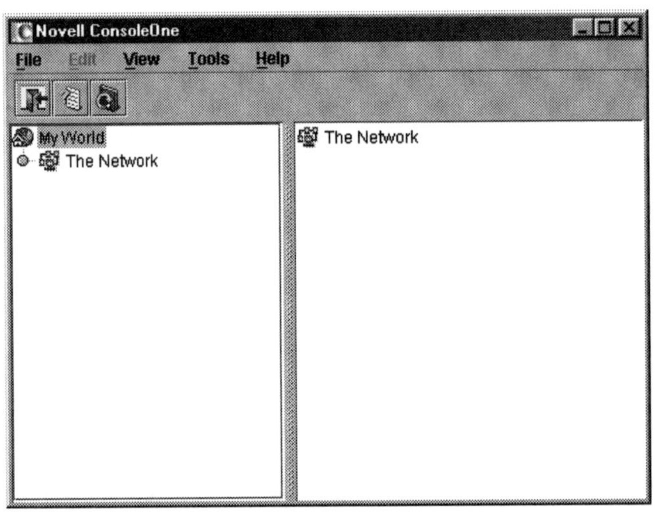

To Add a Group to NDS Using ConsoleOne

1. In the left pane of the ConsoleOne window, double-click the My World selection.

   NOTE The ConsoleOne window resembles the Windows Explorer window. You navigate similarly in both utilities.

2. The next menu displays the Network selection. Click once in the circle directly to the left of this selection. This displays the next menu.

3. From the menu, locate Novell Directory Services. Again, click once in the circle directly to the left of this selection. A menu appears that displays all available trees in the network.

4. In the left pane of the ConsoleOne window, click the circle to the left of the desired tree. This launches a login screen. Enter your administrator user name, password, and context. Click OK.
5. In the left pane of the ConsoleOne window, select the container in which you want to create your group by clicking the circle to the left of the correct container. You are now in the correct container.
6. To create a new group, select the following sequence:

   File ➢ New ➢ Group

7. Enter the group's name in the Group Name field. Select the Define Additional Properties check box and click Create.
8. Enter the information in the appropriate property fields. When complete, click the X button in the upper-left corner of the Properties window. You now see the new group displayed in the NDS tree.

LAB 7: LAB REPORT

DATE ____________________ NAME ________________________________

1. What NDS objects can you create in ConsoleOne?

2. List the three property pages available when creating a group in ConsoleOne.

3. What utility will you use if you need to further define information for objects created in ConsoleOne?

4. From what locations in the network can you launch and use the ConsoleOne utility?

Lab 8: Subnet a Class C IP Address

Objectives

Upon completion of this lab, you will be able to:

1. Recognize a Class C IP address.
2. Subnet a Class C IP address.
3. Determine valid IP address ranges.

Suggested Reading

Chapter 4, pages 135–143, *Network+ Study Guide*, David Groth, Sybex.

Hardware Required

An ample supply of scrap paper.

Software Required

None.

Introduction

TCP/IP is the language of the Internet's massive network. Because of this, if you are in the computer industry today, it is imperative to understand IP addressing. To be able to use the vast world of information available through the Internet, you must be able to configure valid IP address schemes throughout your network. To configure valid IP addresses, you must first recognize the classes and regulations associated with IP addressing.

To use routing technology and to control the traffic flowing through your network, you can use *subnetting*. In subnetting, you modify an IP address range given to an organization and create several smaller network address ranges. This allows you to separate and isolate network traffic, creating greater security and greater throughput of data. This lab introduces the concept of subnetting and allows you to practice using a given IP address scheme.

For this lab, the Class C network address is 204.16.95.0. You have the entire address range for this network. By subnetting, you will create six separate networks. To do this, you will first determine the *subnet mask*. The subnet mask of the Class C address that you are subnetting is the 32-bit number that separates the network identifier from the node identifier. The subnet mask in this lab is written in binary notation as the following:

11111111.11111111.11111111.00000000

In dotted decimal notation it is written as the following:

255.255.255.0

A great tool to determine the subnet mask is the following commonly used table. The top number refers to the subnetted octet's subnet mask. The bottom number is the starting and increment point for subnetting. To determine the number of bits you need to borrow for the subnet mask, look ahead one number and subtract 2.

128	192	224	240	248	252	254	255
128	64	32	16	8	4	2	1

After you determine the subnet mask, you will then determine the six network address ranges that are available.

PROCEDURE

To Determine the Subnet Mask

1. To subnet your network, use the table in the introduction to determine the number of address bits that you will borrow from the fourth octet of the IP address.
2. Document the subnet mask for your network.

To Determine the Valid IP Address Schemes

1. Based on the results of the first exercise of the lab, determine the valid address ranges for your network. Identify the subnet mask for your network.
2. Use binary counting to determine the first valid address range.

> **NOTE** If you are using the first three bits of the host address as part of the network portion, your binary count scheme should look like this: 000, 001, 010, 011, 100, 101, and 111. The remaining five bits will be used for host addressing.

3. Continue with the next network bit scheme and calculate the IP address ranges for the remaining subnetworks.

> **TIP** One way to determine the valid address range is by straight binary counting. If the first three bits of the fourth octet are network segments, as opposed to node segments, write the valid address range out in longhand binary: 11001100.00010000.01011111.000*xxxxx*, where *xxxxx* will span all zeros to all ones. The valid address range will span 204.16.95.0 through 204.16.95.31.

LAB 8: LAB REPORT

DATE ____________________ NAME ____

1. Why is the ability to subnet important?

2. List the advantages of subnetting a network.

3. Explain how you determine the number of node bits you must borrow for network identification to create *x* number of networks.

4. List six of the valid IP address ranges you determined.

Lab 9: Understanding DNS Using DOS Investigation Utilities

Objectives

Upon completion of this lab, you will be able to:

1. Understand the function of a DNS server.
2. Use DOS utilities to understand DNS.
3. Find the results of DNS searches.

Suggested Reading

Chapter 4, pages 147–150, *Network+ Study Guide*, David Groth, Sybex.

Hardware Needed

An operational Windows 95 PC with an active network connection.

Software Needed

None.

Introduction

What if you needed to know the IP address for every location server that you wanted to contact? This would be the equivalent of knowing all of your acquaintances by social security number instead of by name. It is impossible to memorize all of those numbers. Thankfully, that is the job of the DNS server. To access a resource on the Internet, you only need to know the domain name, such as `www.microsoft.com`. The DNS server in your network will resolve this domain name to the IP address. If your network's DNS server cannot resolve the name to an IP address, the server will pass it on to another DNS server for resolution.

The results of the DNS search can be seen with two DOS utilities: *nslookup* and the *Address Resolution Protocol* (ARP). Nslookup is a program that queries Internet domain name servers. Nslookup has two modes: *interactive* and *non-interactive*. Interactive mode allows the user to query domain name servers for information about various hosts and domains or to print a list of hosts in the domain. The syntax for querying DNS servers is as follows:

nslookup [*–option* ...] [*host to find* | – [*server*]].

The non-interactive mode is used to print just the name and requested information for a host or domain.

The information the DNS server uses to resolve name/IP address issues can also be edited. In this lab, you will use both the ARP and the nslookup utilities so you can further understand the job of DNS.

PROCEDURE

To Use nslookup Interactively

1. Open a DOS window on the workstation by using the following sequence:

    Start ➢ Programs ➢ MS-DOS Prompt

2. At the command line, enter the following:

    nslookup

    The nslookup prompt appears.

3. View the current options by entering the following at the command prompt:

    set all

4. Enter this simple command:

    nslookup [*IP address*]

5. Record the IP address of the DNS server.

    TIP Commands may be interrupted at any time by typing the system interrupt character (<Del> by default).

6. Enter **Exit** to leave nslookup.

To Access DNS Information Using the ARP Utility

1. Open a DOS window on your PC by using the following sequence:

    Start ➢ Programs ➢ MS-DOS Prompt

2. Gather the IP address information for your classroom. Ping the workstations in your classroom by typing the following at the prompt:

    ping [*IP address*]

3. In your DOS window, you should receive a message letting you know that your workstation received a reply from the machine with that IP address. If you did not receive the reply message, there are communication problems in your network.

4. At the DOS prompt, type in the following to use the Address Resolution Protocol (ARP) command:

    arp –a

5. Examine the results. You will see the IP address to computer name resolution (see Figure 9.1).

FIGURE 9.1 Sample ARP results

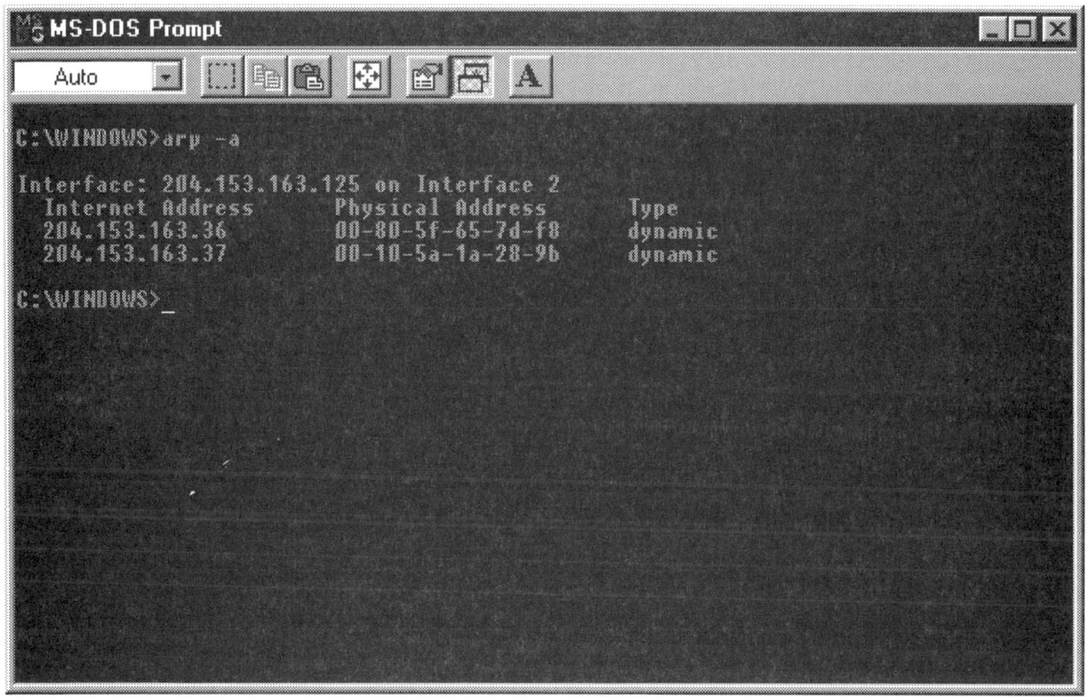

6. Record the results.

7. Close the DOS window.

LAB 9: LAB REPORT

DATE ____________________ NAME ____

1. What is a DNS server?

2. If a DNS server cannot resolve an address conflict, what will it do?

3. What is the purpose of the nslookup utility?

4. What information did you obtain from the arp –a command?

Lab 10: Using netstat and Its Switches

Objectives

Upon completion of this lab, you will be able to:

1. Understand the function of the netstat utility.
2. Understand the information provided by using switches with the netstat command.

Suggested Reading

Chapter 5, pages 174–181, *Network+ Study Guide*, David Groth, Sybex.

Hardware Needed

A functioning Windows 95 workstation with an active network connection.

Software Needed

None.

Introduction

In today's networked world, an understanding of TCP/IP is a necessity. The TCP/IP connections that transmit information through a network can be seen using utilities.

In this lab, you are going to investigate TCP/IP on a different level than in the previous labs by taking a look at the netstat utility and its command switches. The *netstat command* is issued from the Windows 95 command prompt. It displays information about the current protocol and about TCP/IP connections.

The netstat utility has the following parameters:

–a Displays all connections and listening ports.

–e Displays Ethernet statistics. This may be combined with the –s option.

–n Displays addresses and port numbers in numerical form.

–p Shows connections for the protocol specified by protocol. The protocol may be TCP or UDP. If used with the –s option to display per-protocol statistics, the protocol may be TCP, UDP, ICMP, or IP.

–r Displays the contents of the routing table.

–s Displays per-protocol statistics. By default, statistics are shown for TCP, UDP, ICMP, and IP. The –p option may be used to specify a subset of the default.

PROCEDURE

To Examine Workstation IP Connections Using netstat

1. Open a DOS window in your Windows 95 workstation by following this sequence:

   Start ➢ Programs ➢ MS-DOS Prompt

2. At the command prompt, enter the following:

   netstat /?

   You will be given the available netstat parameters.

3. To use and display the current IP connections, type the following:

   netstat –a

4. Record the results.
5. Experiment with the other switches listed in the introduction. Identify the different protocols. Also, take note of the –r switch, which will show you the current routing table.
6. Close the window.

LAB 10: LAB REPORT

DATE ____________________ NAME ____

1. What is the purpose of the netstat utility?

____

____

____

____

2. What is a routing table? What switch do you use to display this?

____

____

____

____

3. What protocols did you see represented while using the –p switch?

____

____

____

____

4. What information is represented when you use the –n switch?

____

____

____

____

Lab 11: Configure an IP Address on a Workstation

Objectives

Upon completion of this lab, you will be able to:

1. Install TCP/IP on a workstation.
2. Configure an IP address on a workstation.
3. Configure a gateway on a workstation.

Suggested Reading

Chapter 4, pages 153–161, *Network+ Study Guide,* David Groth, Sybex.

Hardware Needed

A working PC with Windows 95 installed.

Software Needed

None.

Introduction

For a workstation to communicate with the Internet, you must install the TCP/IP protocol stack, and the workstation must have an IP address. In this lab, you will install the TCP/IP protocol on a Windows 95 workstation and assign the workstation an IP address.

PROCEDURE

To Install the TCP/IP Protocol Stack on a Workstation

1. Open the Network window in the Control Panel by following this sequence:

   Start ➢ Settings ➢ Control Panel ➢ Network

2. The upper portion of the Network window displays the installed components. Verify that TCP/IP has not been installed.
3. Click the Add button beneath the Installed Components window.
4. Choose Protocol from the selection window that appears. Click Add again. Another selection window appears.
5. From the left selection window, choose Microsoft. On the right side, TCP/IP will appear.
6. Click TCP/IP and click OK.

To Enter an IP Address on the Workstation

1. Scroll through the Installed Components window to find the TCP/IP protocol you just installed. Highlight it and click the Properties button directly below it. The Properties window will appear.
2. In the IP Address tab (see Figure 11.1), click the Specify An IP Address button. The grayed-out portion now opens and allows you to enter IP information.
3. Enter the IP address. (The instructor will give you a valid IP address.) Enter the subnet mask in the Subnet Mask field.

FIGURE 11.1 The IP Address tab of the TCP/IP Properties dialog box

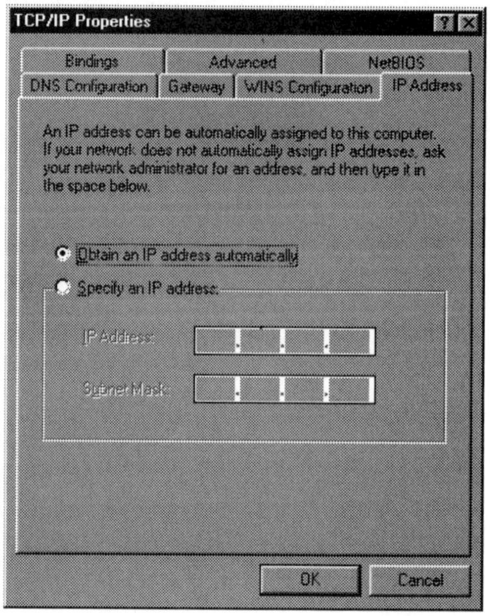

4. Click the Gateway tab (see Figure 11.2). In the New Gateway field, enter the correct gateway address. Click the Add button to the right of the window. In the lower-right corner of the window, click OK.

FIGURE 11.2 The Gateway tab of the TCP/IP Properties dialog box

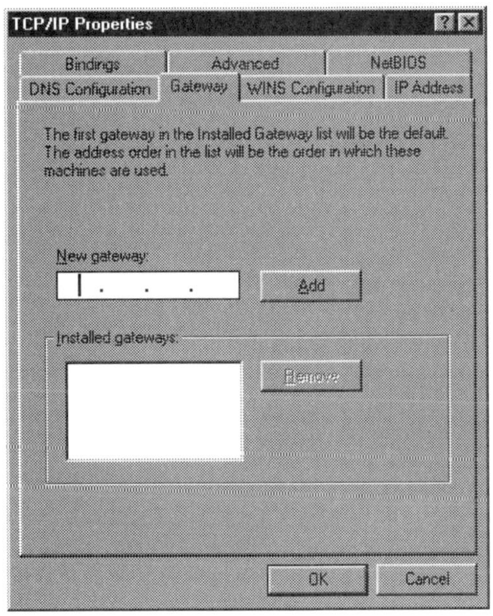

5. To complete the procedure, click OK again. The workstation will reboot.

To Verify the Procedure

1. Open a DOS Prompt window by following this sequence:

   Start ➢ Programs ➢ MS-DOS Prompt

2. Type the following command:

   WINIPCFG

3. Verify the IP configuration of the workstation.

LAB 11: LAB REPORT

DATE ____________________ NAME ____

1. Why do you need a valid IP address for a workstation that connects to the Internet?

____

____

____

____

2. How is the subnet mask determined?

____

____

____

____

3. What is a gateway?

____

____

____

____

4. What information did you obtain from the WINIPCFG DOS utility?

____

____

____

____

Lab 12: Download a File Using FTP

Objectives

Upon completion of this lab, you will be able to:

1. Understand FTP.
2. Download a file using FTP.

Suggested Reading

Chapter 4, page 130, and Chapter 5, pages 188–192, *Network+ Study Guide,* David Groth, Sybex.

Hardware Needed

A functional Windows 95 workstation with active Internet connectivity.

Software Needed

None.

Introduction

The protocol in the TCP/IP protocol suite that allows you to transfer simple files using the Internet is called *FTP* (File Transfer Protocol). FTP is a transfer program for TCP/IP environments that is implemented at the Application layer of the OSI model.

You have probably noticed the option to download a file from an HTTP or an FTP site when downloading a driver from a manufacturer's Web site. The files found on the FTP server cannot be accessed directly; the entire file must be transferred from the FTP server to the local server. In this lab, you will download a file from Novell's FTP site to the local machine.

PROCEDURE

To Connect to the FTP Site

1. Turn on the PC. It will boot to the Windows 95 Desktop.
2. From the Desktop, launch a Web browser. You can use either Microsoft's Internet Explorer or Novell's Netscape Navigator. Whichever you choose, the browser will open to your home page.
3. Locate Novell's FTP site. At the request line, type:

   ftp://ftp.novell.com

4. The home page for Novell's FTP site will open.

To Download a File Using FTP

1. Explore and become familiar with Novell's FTP site and with their Web (HTTP) site.
2. Locate a downloadable file. Underneath the text at the top of the screen, there is a list of the downloadable files available on the site.
3. Click the desired file. A Save As screen will appear. Determine where you want to save the file and click OK.
4. The file transfer time depends upon the size of the file. After the download is complete, press OK.
5. Close the Browser window.

To Verify That the Download Was Successful

1. From the Windows 95 Desktop, open My Computer.
2. Navigate to the location where you saved the file from ftp.novell.com.
3. Open the file to verify that the download was successful.

LAB 12: LAB REPORT

DATE ____________________ NAME ____

1. On which layer of the OSI model does the FTP application reside?

____

____

____

____

2. What is the difference between an FTP site and an HTTP site?

____

____

____

____

3. To connect to the FTP site, what command do you use at the browser's request line?

____

____

____

____

4. List three differences you noticed between Novell's FTP site and the Novell HTTP site.

____

____

____

____

Lab 13: Find the Routed Path to an Internet Destination Using tracert

Objectives

Upon completion of this lab, you will be able to:

1. Determine the routed path to a destination on the Internet.
2. Learn how tracert can be used in troubleshooting.
3. Understand how signals are routed across the Internet.

Suggested Reading

Chapter 5, pages 198–199, *Network+ Study Guide*, David Groth, Sybex.

Hardware Needed

An operational Windows 95 PC with Internet connectivity.

Software Needed

None.

Introduction

It may seem like magic that you can send a mail message over the Internet and it can be received across the globe in a matter of minutes. But, the Internet is not magic. To understand how it transmits data, you must understand routing. To send a message over the Internet, the signal is passed from router to router until it is eventually sent to the router on the receiving node's network.

In this lab, you will use the tracert DOS utility to look at the route of a signal as you send it to a destination on the network. The lab will show step by step how information is routed to its destination on the Internet.

PROCEDURE

Use the tracert Utility to Determine the Route to a Destination

1. Turn on the Windows 95 workstation.
2. Launch a DOS window by following this sequence:

   Start ➢ Programs ➢ MS-DOS Prompt
3. At the command line, type the following:

   tracert /?

   This command will give you a listing of the available options that you can include with the tracert command.
4. At the command line, type the following:

   tracert www.novell.com
5. View the results. Notice that the FQDN (Fully Qualified Domain Name) was resolved to the IP address.
6. At the command line, type the following:

   tracert www.novell.com –h [*maximum hops*]

   Note if this command changed the route that was taken to the desired destination.
7. At the command line, type the following:

   tracert www.novell.com –w [*timeout*]

   Note if this command changed the route that was taken to the desired destination.

Understanding the tracert Screen

1. Note the first column on your screen. (It will look like Figure 13.1.) This column specifies the hop number of the destination route.

NOTE A hop is a stop at a hardware location, such as a server or a router. The maximum number of hops to a location is generally 16.

2. Note the second column on your screen. This specifies the time in milliseconds that is required to reach the next destination.

3. Note the third column on your screen. This specifies the IP address and host name of the servicing system.

FIGURE 13.1 Sample tracert output

```
C:\>tracert www.yahoo.com
Tracing route to www10.yahoo.com [204.71.200.75]
over a maximum of 30 hops:

  1   110 ms    96 ms   107 ms  fgo1.corpcomm.net [209.74.93.10]
  2    96 ms   126 ms    95 ms  someone.corpcomm.net [209.74.93.1]
  3   113 ms   119 ms   112 ms  Serial5-1-1.GW2.MSP1.alter.net [157.130.100.185]
  4   133 ms   123 ms   126 ms  152.ATM3-0.XR2.CHI6.ALTER.NET [146.188.209.126]
  5   176 ms   133 ms   129 ms  290.ATM2-0.TR2.CHI4.ALTER.NET [146.188.209.10]
  6   196 ms   184 ms   218 ms  106.ATM7-0.TR2.SCL1.ALTER.NET [146.188.136.162]
  7   182 ms   187 ms   187 ms  298.ATM7-0.XR2.SJC1.ALTER.NET [146.188.146.61]
  8   204 ms   176 ms   186 ms  192.ATM3-0-0.SAN-JOSE9-GW.ALTER.NET [146.188.144.133]
  9   202 ms   198 ms   212 ms  atm3-0-622M.cr1.sjc.globalcenter.net [206.57.16.17]
 10   209 ms   202 ms   195 ms  pos3-1-155M.br4.SJC.globalcenter.net [206.132.150.98]
 11   190 ms     *      191 ms  pos0-0-0-155M.hr3.SNV.globalcenter.net [206.251.5.93]
 12   195 ms   188 ms   188 ms  pos4-1-0-155M.hr2.SNV.globalcenter.net [206.132.150.206]
 13   198 ms   202 ms   197 ms  www10.yahoo.com [204.71.200.75]

Trace complete.
```

LAB 13: LAB REPORT

DATE ____________________ NAME ____

1. What is the purpose of the tracert utility?

____

____

____

____

2. How can you use the tracert utility to troubleshoot a problem with sending data over a WAN?

____

____

____

____

3. What is a hop? What is the maximum number of hops required to reach a destination address?

____

____

____

____

4. What differences did you note when applying the different command options of the tracert utility?

____

____

____

____

Lab 14: Install and Configure a Network Interface Card in a Workstation

Objectives

Upon completion of this lab, you will be able to:

1. Install a network interface card into a workstation.
2. Configure the network interface card in the workstation.
3. Test the network interface card at the workstation.

Suggested Reading

Chapter 6, pages 237–246, *Network+ Study Guide*, David Groth, Sybex.

Hardware Needed

1. An operational Windows 95 workstation.
2. A compatible network interface card.

Software Needed

1. A Windows 95 Installation CD-ROM.
2. The software driver for the network interface card that is to be installed.

Introduction

The best network layout and cabling scheme is worthless if you don't have the proper *network interface card* (NIC). The NIC is the component in the PC that receives the information being sent on the network and puts it into a transmittable scheme. It also receives incoming transmissions and transforms them into a language that the computer can understand.

There are numerous types of NICs available. The network administrator determines the speed, adaptability, and type of card that will best fit the network's needs. This is determined by the cabling on the network, the speed throughout the network, and the expected growth of the network.

Another important component is the software adapter driver, which allows the PC to communicate with the NIC. Generally, the NIC manufacturer's Web site will provide you with the most recent software for your card. It is a good idea to use the most recent software available when installing any hardware component into your PC.

PROCEDURE

To Install the Network Interface Card

1. Shut down the computer by following this sequence:

   Start ➢ Shut Down ➢ Shut Down The Computer

2. Turn off the power and unplug the PC's power cord.

   TIP Try to practice good Electrostatic Discharge (ESD) prevention measures when handling internal components of your computer. Use grounding wires and static resistant pads beneath the PC. Also, transport the cards in static-shielded bags. The effects of ESD include degraded performance of the computer or failure of its components.

3. Remove any screws holding the case on the computer. Remove the case.
4. Locate the slot to install the NIC. Insert the card into the slot. When inserting it, do not rock the card back and forth. Apply direct and even pressure on the card to push it into the slot.
5. Screw the card into position using the grounding screws.
6. Reassemble the PC.

To Configure the Network Interface Card in the PC

1. Plug the power cord back into the PC. Turn on the workstation and let the system boot.
2. Your system may detect the new hardware. If this is the case, the system will ask you for driver software to complete the installation. When the request for a driver comes on-screen, insert the driver software disk and select the Have Disk option. The installation will automatically occur.
3. If the system does not detect the hardware, you will need to install the card manually. To do so, go to the Control Panel of the workstation by following this sequence:

   Start ➢ Settings ➢ Control Panel

4. Choose the Add New Hardware option. In the window that appears, choose the Next option.
5. The next window will offer to allow Windows to find the new hardware. Select No and click Next.
6. From the device list, choose the Network Adapters option. A selection window appears with common interface cards. Insert the disk that contains the software configuration for the card. Click the Have Disk button.
7. The system will copy the necessary information from the configuration disk. Choose Next to install the card.
8. You may need to provide files from the Windows 95 CD-ROM. If this is requested, insert the disk and choose Next. The necessary files will be copied to the workstation.
9. The setup is now complete. Choose Finish. The workstation will reboot.

To Verify That the Network Interface Card Is Installed Properly

1. After the workstation boots up, open a DOS window by following this sequence:

   Start ➢ Programs ➢ MS-DOS Prompt

2. To ping your workstation, type the following command at the prompt:

   ping 127.0.0.1

   NOTE The IP address 127.0.0.1 is a troubleshooting utility. When you ping this IP address, you are verifying the operability of the card installed in your workstation.

3. You should receive reply text on the screen. If you do not see this, there is a problem with the configuration of the card or a problem with the card itself.

LAB 14: LAB REPORT

DATE ____________________ NAME ____

1. What is the function of a network interface card in a PC?

2. What are the advantages of using the most recent software when installing a hardware component into a PC?

3. How can you test that the NIC is working properly?

4. List some other ways to test that an NIC is functioning properly.

Lab 15: Install a Software Patch on an Operating System

Objectives

Upon completion of this lab, you will be able to:

1. Find the most recent patch for a Windows 95 workstation.
2. Install the most recent patch for a Windows 95 workstation.

Suggested Reading

Chapter 6, pages 246–248 and 446–448, *Network+ Study Guide*, David Groth, Sybex.

Hardware Needed

1. A functional Windows 95 workstation with Internet connectivity.
2. A blank 3.5" floppy disk.

Software Needed

None.

Introduction

Software vendors are continuously fixing and updating their products. The updates to the software can include new products, better support for existing options of the software, or fixes for glitches that existed in the software at the time of its release.

These software updates are offered on the Web sites of the major players in operating system software, such as Novell and Microsoft. Other vendors, such as makers of network interface cards, modems, or other hardware devices, also offer updated drivers for their products on their Web sites. You can connect to the Web site and download these updates.

In this lab, you will connect to Microsoft's support site and download the most recent software patch for the Windows 95 operating system. You will then install this patch onto your workstations.

PROCEDURE

To Download the Most Recent Software Patch

1. Open a Web browser on your workstation. You can use either Microsoft's Internet Explorer or Novell's Netscape Navigator.
2. At the request line, enter the following:

   www.microsoft.com

3. Click the hyperlink to Microsoft's download site.
4. To specify the Windows 95 operating system, click the Search button.
5. Several options appear in the list. Scroll down the list and find the Windows 95 Service Pack 1 option (see Figure 15.1).

FIGURE 15.1 Choosing an option from the Microsoft Download Center

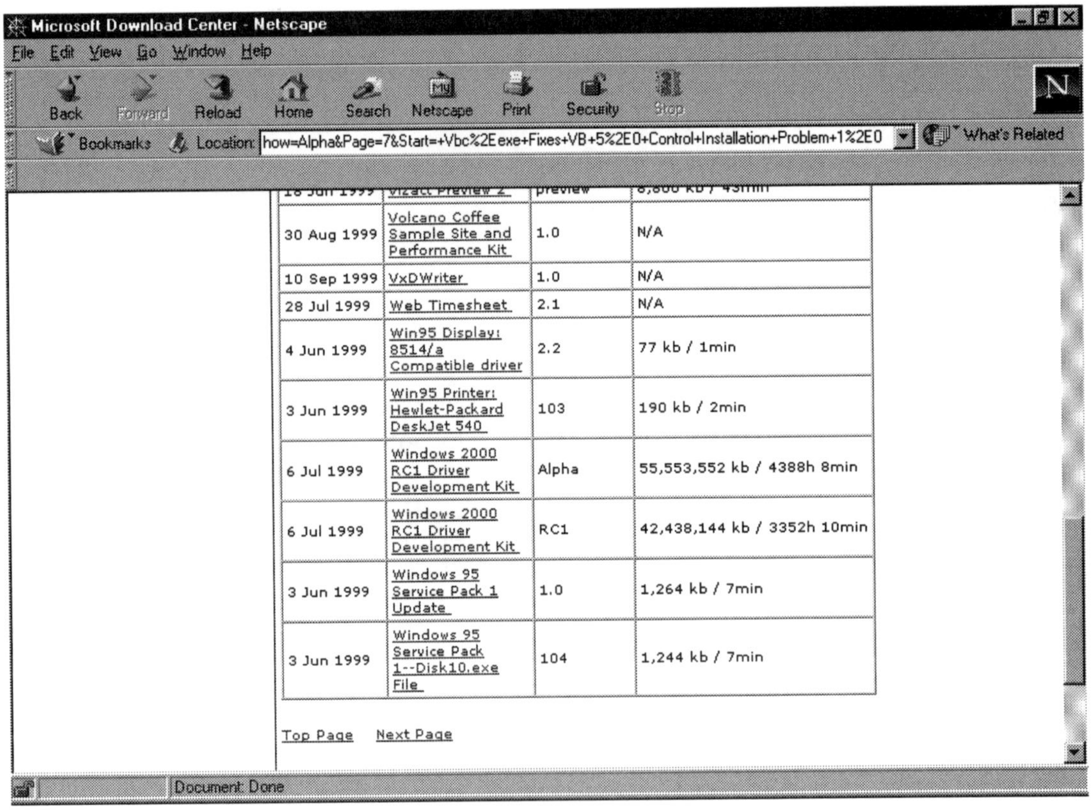

6. Click the hyperlink next to this option. A downloadable file appears.

7. Insert the floppy disk into your PC. Click the downloadable file. Specify your A: drive to save the file to.

NOTE You also have the option to save the file to hard disk instead of on a floppy.

8. Download the file. The file's download time depends on the speed of your Internet connection. You should now have the INSTALL.EXE file on the floppy.

To Install Service Pack 1

1. From the Windows 95 Desktop, open My Computer.

2. Double-click the A: drive.

3. Double-click the INSTALL.EXE file.

4. A window appears letting your know that the file will install the service pack onto the workstation. Click OK.

5. A software agreement will appear. Read the agreement. In the lower-left corner of the License Agreement screen, click the I Agree button.

6. The software will be copied to your workstation. This may take a few minutes. After the files are installed, the Completion screen appears. Click OK.

7. To complete the installation, it is necessary to restart the computer by following this sequence:

   Start ➢ Restart The Computer

LAB 15: LAB REPORT

DATE ____________________ NAME ____

1. Why do you need to install updated drivers or support packs for components of the network?

____

____

____

____

2. Where do you find the most recent support packs for Microsoft products?

____

____

____

____

3. What is the filename that installs the updated software to the Windows 95 workstation?

____

____

____

____

4. What is the final step necessary to complete the update of your operating system?

____

____

____

____

Lab 16: Install and Configure an External Modem

Objectives

Upon completion of this lab, you will be able to:

1. Install a modem in your Windows 95 workstation.
2. Configure the modem in your Windows 95 workstation.

Suggested Reading

Chapter 7, pages 255–266, *Network+ Study Guide,* David Groth, Sybex.

Hardware Needed

1. A functional Windows 95 workstation.
2. An external modem.
3. A modem cable.
4. A phone cable.

Software Needed

1. A Windows 95 Install CD-ROM.
2. If needed, software for the modem installation.

Introduction

The ability to connect to a remote network through your computer requires the use of a modem. A *modem* allows you to dial into your local ISP (Internet Service Provider) to connect to the Internet or to dial into your office so that you can work from home. In order to make these connections, you need to install a modem on your PC.

A modem (modulator/demodulator) converts the digital signal that your computer sends into an analog signal that is carried over a POTS (Plain Old Telephone Service) or a PSTN (Public Switched Telephone Network) line. At the receiving end, this analog signal is reconverted into a digital signal that the computer can understand.

There are various makes and models of modems. They range in transmission speed from a 2400 baud rate to 56K (currently the fastest connection speed available for a modem). The actual speed of transmission also depends on the quality of the phone line; some lines are not "clean" enough to support the highest speeds of transmission.

In this lab, you will attach and configure a modem to your Windows 95 workstation. You'll also learn how to install any modem to a PC.

PROCEDURE

To Attach a Modem to a PC

1. Turn off the computer.
2. Move the workstation so you can see the back of it. Find the Com 1 port on the back of the PC. Connect the modem cable to this port and tighten the screws on the cable.
3. Attach the other end of the modem cable to the modem's communication port. Again, tighten the screws on the cable.
4. Find the phone cable. At the back of the modem, there are two ports: one labeled "Phone" and the other labeled "Line." Connect the phone cable to the Line port.
5. Turn on the computer.

To Configure a Modem

1. At the Windows 95 Desktop, click the Start button.
2. Go to the Control Panel by following this sequence:

   Start ➢ Settings ➢ Control Panel

3. In the Control Panel, double-click the Modems option.
4. A window appears. Click the Add button.
5. An installation wizard will launch. Choose Other and click Next.
6. The next screen allows Windows 95 to find the modem and install it for you. Select the check box that allows you to install the modem manually. Click Next.
7. A list of common modems appears. Find the manufacturer and model of the modem connected to your PC. If it is not listed, select the Have Disk check box.
8. If your modem is not listed, install the modem installation software into your workstation. The wizard will bring you to the Installation screen and will install the modem from the disk.
9. If you did find the modem on the list, click Next.
10. From the next screen, choose the Com 1 port. Click Next.
11. Windows will install the modem. When this is complete, click Finish. You now see the modem you installed in the Installed box of the Modem screen.
12. Click Close.

To Test a Modem

1. From the Windows 95 Desktop, select the following sequence:

   Start ➢ Settings ➢ Control Panel

2. In the Control Panel window, double-click the Modems icon.
3. The Modems Properties window will open. At the top of the window, click the Diagnostics tab.
4. Highlight the COM port that your modem is on (see Figure 16.1). Click the More Info button.

FIGURE 16.1 The Dianostics tab of the Modems Properties window

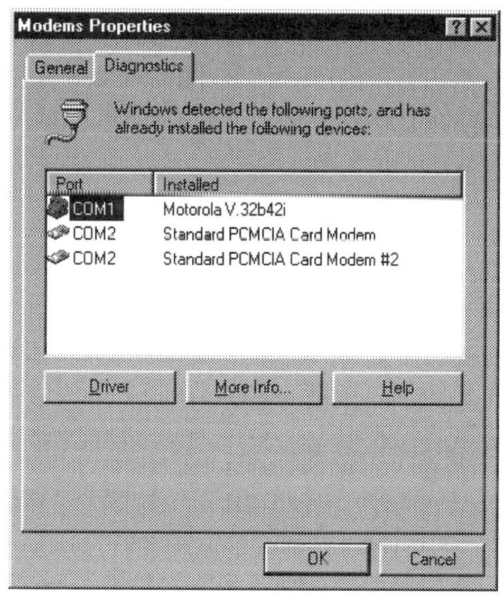

5. The system will run a diagnostic check on the modem. If Windows 95 can communicate with the modem, the modem driver is functioning properly.

LAB 16: LAB REPORT

DATE ____________________ NAME ____

1. List three reasons that a PC needs a modem.

____

____

____

____

2. Currently, what is the fastest connection speed available via a modem?

____

____

____

____

3. What factors determine the connection speed of a modem?

____

____

____

____

4. Where can you get updated software for a modem?

____

____

____

____

Lab 17: Create a User Login Script in a NetWare Network

Objectives

Upon completion of this lab, you will be able to:

1. Create a User login script.
2. Understand the scripting language of the login script.
3. Test the login script.

Suggested Reading

Chapter 8, pages 286–287 and 300–302, *Network+ Study Guide*, David Groth, Sybex.

Hardware Needed

A functional Windows 95 workstation attached to a NetWare 5 network.

Software Needed

NetWare Administrator attached to a NetWare 5 network.

Introduction

The ability to customize and control the workstation environment for NetWare users is very powerful. You can send messages to your users, define network connections, and connect users to different peripheral devices on the network with login scripts.

NetWare 5 login scripts are comprised of four different levels of scripting. The first level is the *Container login script* where you define the environment for the entire container. In this script, you can create IF statements that allow the administrator to further customize the user's environment.

The next scripts to run are the *Profile login scripts*. These are for select users who need special environment settings.

Next, is the *Default login script*. This script cannot be edited and will set up generic environmental variables for all users who do not define a User login script. When no User login script is configured, the Default login script will run.

The last login script to run is the *User login script*. It is designed to automate a user's special settings.

In this lab, you will create a User login script. You will also learn basic scripting language for a NetWare 5 environment.

PROCEDURE

To Launch NetWare Administrator

1. From the Windows 95 Desktop, double-click Network Neighborhood.
2. Double-click the Entire Network option. From the next option screen, choose NetWare Servers.
3. Find the appropriate server. Choose the SYS: volume on the NetWare server.
4. Choose the following path to NetWare Administrator:

   SYS: ➢ Public ➢ Win32 ➢ Nwadm32

5. Double-click the NWADM32 option. NetWare Administrator will launch.

To Create a User Login Script

1. Find a user object in NetWare Administrator.
2. Right-click the USER object. From the menu options that appear on the right, choose Details.
3. The Details screen appears. On the right side of the Details screen, click the Login Script button. A blank Login Script screen will appear (see Figure 17.1).

FIGURE 17.1 A blank login script

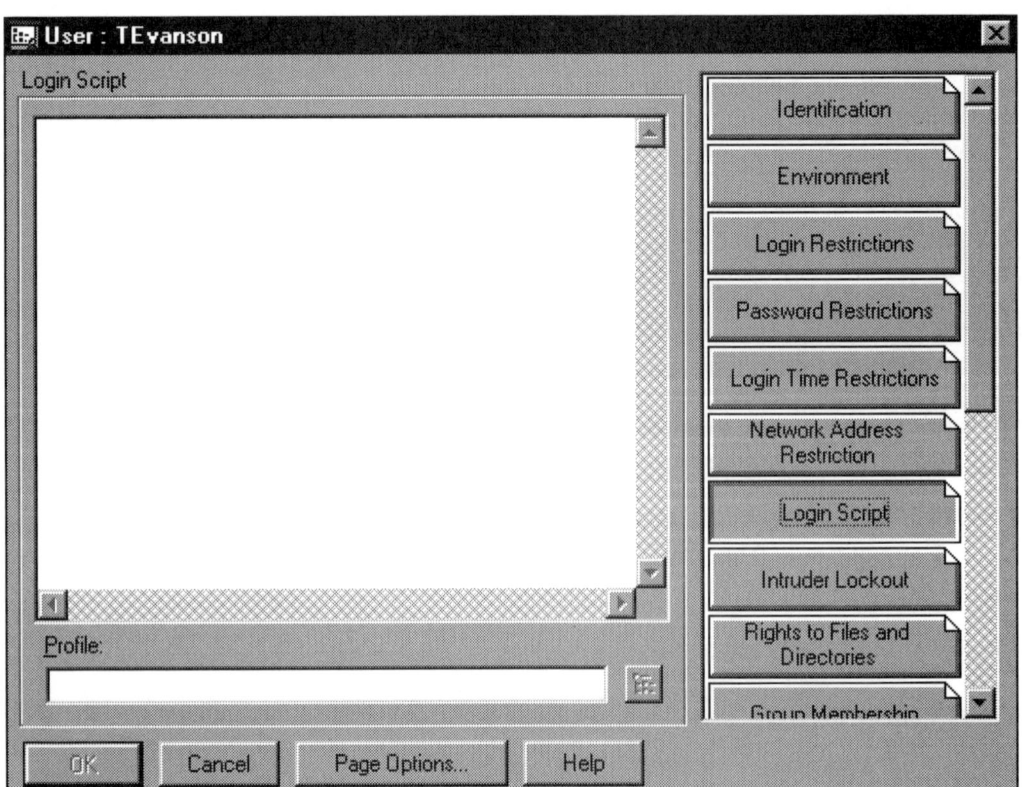

4. You will now create the login script. For this lab, you will set variables to map a network drive, display a greeting, and sound phasers at login. To do this, use the following script:

   MAP G:=*SERVERNAME*:SYS\PUBLIC

   WRITE "GOOD %GREETING_TIME, %LOGIN_NAME"

   FIRE PHASERS 5

5. Click OK.
6. Note the username of the user you just created a login script for and verify that no password is required for login.

To Test a User Login Script

1. In the lower-left corner of the Windows 95 Desktop screen, right-click the red N option in the System Tray.
2. From the menu screen that appears, select NetWare Login. The Login screen will appear.
3. Login as the user you created in Step 6 of the previous exercise.
4. Take note of the login script that runs. If the previous exercise was completed correctly, you should see the greeting, and the G: drive will be mapped to the PUBLIC directory of the SYS: volume. You should also hear 5 beeps as the login script runs.

LAB 17: LAB REPORT

DATE ____________________ NAME ____

1. List three parameters that you can set with a login script.

2. What are the four login scripts available with NetWare 5?

3. When you create a User login script, which of the other login scripts is automatically omitted?

4. Which of the four login scripts cannot be edited?

Lab 18: Edit a Windows Login Script on a Windows NT Workstation

Objectives

Upon completion of this lab, you will be able to:

1. Create a batch file to use as a login script.
2. Configure User Manager for Domains to use the login script .BAT file.
3. Test the login script.

Suggested Reading

Chapter 8, pages 286–287 and 300–302, *Network+ Study Guide*, David Groth, Sybex.

Hardware Needed

A functional Windows NT workstation.

Software Needed

User Manager for Domains installed on the NT workstation.

Introduction

Network administrators commonly create and use login scripts. Login scripts save time by allowing you to customize the network user's environment without having to visit each workstation individually.

In this lab, you will learn how to create and customize a login script for your Windows NT network users.

PROCEDURES

To Create the .BAT File with Login Script Instructions

1. Boot your computer to the Windows NT Desktop.
2. To open Notepad, a text editor that is included in the Windows NT environment, follow this sequence:

   Start ➢ Programs ➢ Accessories ➢ Notepad

3. Type the login script command text into Notepad. For this lab, we will use a simple command text:

   net use H:\\[*servername*]\[*sharename*]

> **NOTE** More login script commands are available. You can find the syntax rules for these commands on Microsoft's Web site at `www.microsoft.com`.

4. Save this file as C:\LOGIN.BAT. To do this, click the File option at the top of the screen. Choose Save As. Find the root of the C:\ drive and type the filename. Click Save.
5. Close Notepad by clicking the File menu and selecting Exit.
6. In the upper-left corner of the Desktop, find My Computer.
7. Double-click My Computer. Then, double-click the C:\ drive. Verify that the LOGIN.BAT file was saved there.
8. Close My Computer by clicking the X button in the upper-left corner of the window.

To Implement the LOGIN.BAT File as the Login Script Command Text

1. Open User Manager for Domains.
2. Find the user you want to use this login script for. Document the username and the password for this user. You will use this information to test the login script.
3. Enter the properties of the USER object.
4. Click the profile for the USER object.
5. In the Profile screen, click the Login Script option.
6. In the window that appears, specify the path to the login script. Type in the following:

   C:\LOGIN.BAT

7. Click OK to save the LOGIN.BAT file as the login script.
8. Close User Manager for Domains.

To Test the Login Script

1. On the Windows NT Desktop, click the Start button.
2. From the menu, select Shutdown.
3. A window appears. Select the "Close all programs and login as a different user" option.
4. Click OK.
5. The system will log off the original user and bring you back to the Login screen. Log in as the user you modified in the second exercise of this lab.
6. From the Desktop, open My Computer.
7. The G:\ drive appears. Double-click this drive to verify that you are at the specified location in the file system.
8. Close My Computer by clicking the X button in the upper-left corner of the window.

LAB 18: LAB REPORT

DATE ____________________ NAME ____

1. What is the purpose of creating a login script?

2. Which type of program do you use to create the parameters for the login script?

3. Where do you specify the file to use for the User login script? In which program do you do this?

4. List two ways to test that you successfully implemented the login script.

Lab 19: Map a Network Drive on a Windows NT Workstation

Objectives

Upon completion of this lab, you will be able to:

1. Map a network drive on a Windows NT workstation using a login script.
2. Map a network drive on a Windows NT workstation using Network Neighborhood.
3. Verify that the drive mapping is connected.

Suggested Reading

Chapter 8, pages 296–298, *Network+ Study Guide*, David Groth, Sybex.

Hardware Needed

A functional Windows NT workstation attached to an NT network.

Software Needed

None.

Introduction

Shortcuts save time. And any time that network administrators can save is a great advantage. One time-saving technique is mapping a network drive. A mapped network drive is analogous to a preset button on your car stereo. When you push a preset button, you are automatically connected to one of your favorite radio stations. If you had to scan through the channels to find this station, that would require extra time and effort.

The same goes for mapping a network drive. Often-used locations in the file system can be "preset." Selecting a preset option will immediately connect you to your favorite folder or directory.

Home directories, application directories, and shared folders are commonly mapped so that the users can easily locate them. In this lab, you will map a network drive through a login script and through Network Neighborhood.

PROCEDURE

To Map a Network Drive Using a Login Script

1. Boot the Windows NT workstation to the Desktop.
2. Open Notepad using the following sequence:

    Start ➢ Programs ➢ Accessories ➢ Notepad

3. Type the login script command text into Notepad. Type the following:

    net use K:*servernamesharename***

4. Save this file as **C:\LOGIN.BAT** by following this sequence:

    File ➢ Save As

    Find the root of the C:\ drive and type the filename. Click Save.

5. Close Notepad by following this sequence:

    File ➢ Exit

6. In the upper-left corner of the Desktop, find My Computer. Double-click My Computer.
7. Double-click the C:\ drive. Verify that the LOGIN.BAT file was saved there.
8. Close My Computer.
9. Open User Manager for Domains on the workstation by following this sequence:

    Start ➢ Programs ➢ User Manager for Domains

10. Find the user account you are using in this lab.
11. Go to the Properties window of the user account.
12. In the Properties window, select the Profile tab.
13. In the Profile tab, specify the login script as the following:

    C:\LOGIN.BAT

14. Close User Manager for Domains.

To Map a Network Drive Using Network Neighborhood

1. Boot the Windows NT workstation to the Desktop.
2. Right-click the Network Neighborhood icon.
3. A menu will appear to the right of the icon. Choose the Map A Network Drive option.

4. A Drive Mapping screen appears. From the top drop-down menu, select drive letter L: for the drive mapping.

5. To the right of the next drop-down menu, click the Browse button.

6. Browse the network until you find the desired file system location for the drive mapping. Double-click this location.

7. The desired file system location appears in the window. Directly beneath this window is the Reconnect At Login option. Click this option. A check mark will appear.

8. Click OK.

To Verify the Drive Mapping

1. From the Windows NT Desktop, follow this sequence:

   Start ➢ Shutdown ➢ Close All Programs And Log In As A Different User

2. Log into the computer with the user account modified in the first exercise of the lab.

3. From the Windows NT Desktop, double-click the My Computer option. You will see the drive letters K: and L: that you specified in the mapping procedure.

LAB 19: LAB REPORT

DATE ____________________ NAME ____

1. What is the purpose of mapping a network drive?

2. List three advantages of using the mapping feature in a Windows network.

3. What option do you need to specify to permanently assign the drive letter to the specified file location?

4. Does the letter you attach when mapping a drive have any significance?

Lab 20: Map a Network Drive in a NetWare Network

Objectives

Upon completion of this lab, you will be able to:

1. Map a network drive using Network Neighborhood.
2. Map a network drive using the tools available in the System Tray.
3. Map a network drive using a login script.
4. Test the success of the drive mapping.

Suggested Reading

Chapter 8, pages 296–298, *Network+ Study Guide,* David Groth, Sybex.

Hardware Needed

A functional Windows 95 workstation attached to a NetWare 5 network.

Software Needed

NetWare Administrator.

Introduction

Most users want a network environment that is easy to use. One technique that makes using network resources easier is mapping network drives. Mapping network drives allows you to preset commonly used directories in the file system.

There are several ways to map a drive in a NetWare 5 environment. In this lab, you will map a drive using three different methods: using a User login script, using Network Neighborhood, and using the tools in the System Tray.

PROCEDURE

To Map a Network Drive Using a User Login Script

1. From the Windows 95 workstation, launch NetWare Administrator. NetWare Administrator is located in the SYS:\PUBLIC\WIN32 directory on the NetWare server.

2. Browse the NDS tree for the USER object you are using for NetWare login in this class.

3. Right-click the USER object and select Details from the menu that appears.

4. The Details window appears. Note the username and the password of the USER object. You will need this information later to test the success of this exercise.

5. Along the right side of the window, there is an option menu. Click the Login Script button (see Figure 20.1).

FIGURE 20.1 The Login Script button

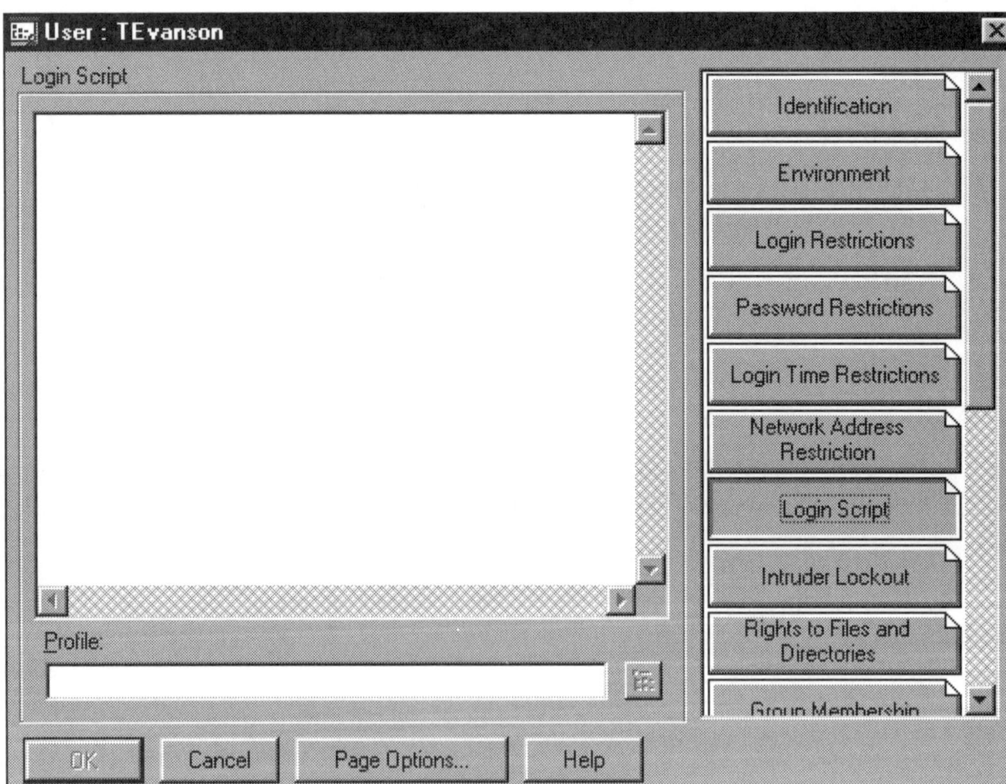

6. An empty window appears. Type the following text:

   map s:=SYS:PUBLIC\WIN32

7. To save this information, click OK.
8. Close NetWare Administrator by clicking the X button in the upper-right corner of the window.

To Map a Network Drive Using Network Neighborhood

1. In the Windows 95 Desktop, right-click the Network Neighborhood icon.
2. A menu appears. Select the Novell Map Network Drive option.
3. The Map Drive window will appear (see Figure 20.2). The top option is Device. Click the drop-down arrow next to the Device option to display the drive letters.

FIGURE 20.2 The Map Drive window

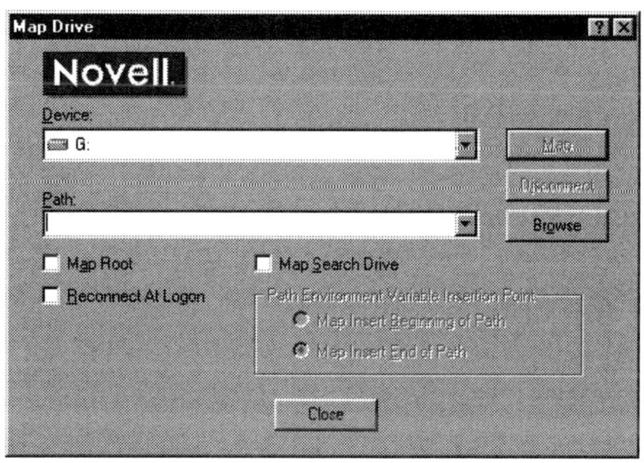

4. Select T: from the list.
5. The next option is labeled Path. Click the Browse button to the right of this option.
6. Browse your NetWare server's network and find the SYS:PUBLIC\WIN32 path.
7. Click OK. This path will appear in the Path option.
8. Three selection options appear below the Path option. Click the Reconnect At Login check box.

> **NOTE** There are two other options. The Map Root option allows you to stop a user from walking up the file system, as this can potentially threaten the security of your file system. The Map As Search Drive option sets a path as a search drive, which allows the system to search the folder to answer command requests from the user. Neither of these options is necessary for this lab.

9. In the upper-right corner of this window, click the Map button. The drive you specified will now be mapped.

To Map a Network Drive Using the System Tray

1. Close all windows that are open on the Windows 95 workstation.
2. In the lower-right corner of your screen, there is a red *N*. This is your System Tray, where you can see the tools available to your system.
3. Right-click the red *N* located in the System Tray.
4. From the menu that appears, choose the Novell Map Network Drive option.
5. A mapping window will appear. The top option is Device. Click the drop-down arrow to display the drive letters.
6. Select U: from the list.
7. The next option is Path. Click the Browse button to the right of this option.
8. Browse your network's NetWare server and follow the SYS:PUBLIC\WIN32 path.
9. Click OK. This path will appear in the Path option.
10. Three selection options appear below the Path option. Click the Reconnect At Login check box.
11. In the upper-right corner of this window, click the Map button. The drive you specified will now be mapped.

To Verify the Drive Mapping

1. From the Windows 95 Desktop, click the Start button.
2. A menu appears. Select the Shutdown option.
3. The Shutdown window lists several options. Choose the "Close all programs and log in as a different user" option.
4. When the Login screen appears, login in as the user you noted in step 4 of the first exercise in this lab.
5. Double-click the My Computer icon. Note the S:, T:, and U: drives. Search these paths to determine if they are mapped to the correct location in your file system.

LAB 20: LAB REPORT

DATE ____________________ NAME ____

1. List three ways to map a drive in a NetWare network.

____

____

____

____

2. When using the User login script to map a network drive, where do you enter the mapping path?

____

____

____

____

3. When you are providing device and path information in the mapping screen, what do the Map Root and Map As Search Drive options mean?

____

____

____

____

4. What is another way to test the success of the drive mapping request that you created?

____

____

____

____

Lab 21: Add and Change Security Rights in a Windows NT Network

Objectives

Upon completion of this lab, you will be able to:

1. Use Windows Explorer to add directory rights for a group in a Windows NT network.
2. Use Windows Explorer to edit directory rights for a group in a Windows NT network.

Suggested Reading

Chapter 9, *Network+ Study Guide,* David Groth, Sybex.

Hardware Needed

An operational Windows NT workstation attached to a Windows NT network.

Software Needed

Windows Explorer.

Introduction

For a network administrator, the security of the network is of the utmost importance because the integrity of the data in a network is only as secure as the security that surrounds it. To maintain security efficiently, network administrators use groups to grant access to network resources.

It is the administrator's job to assign each group the appropriate permissions to each resource. The permissions granted at the directory level determine where a user, or group of users, is able to edit, delete, view, or read information. Network administrators can also grant a group no access to a particular location in the file system. Although it is preferable to grant rights through groups, administrators can assign account permissions through individual users, as well. To edit rights in a Windows NT network, administrators use the Windows Explorer utility.

In this lab, you will learn the necessary tools to edit file system security in a Windows NT network. You will focus on editing file system rights at the group level.

PROCEDURE

To Add File System Security to a Group in Windows Explorer

1. Launch Windows Explorer on the Windows NT workstation by following this sequence:

   Start ➢ Programs ➢ Windows Explorer

2. Browse through the network to find the desired file system location. Highlight the directory where you are going to grant rights for the group.
3. From the Security menu at the top of the screen, select Permissions.
4. At the bottom of the screen, click the Add… button. Double-click the group you would like to add directory rights to.
5. This group will now be displayed in the Name window. Highlight the group you just added.
6. At the bottom of the screen in the Type Of Access window, click the down arrow to display the available rights to the directory. Select the appropriate security level for the group you are adding directory rights to.
7. Above the Name window, there are two options available: "Replace permissions on subdirectories" and "Replace permissions on existing files." Select both of these check boxes. These options guarantee that the directory rights that you choose will apply to all subdirectories of the chosen directory.
8. Click OK. The system will set up the appropriate security. This may take a few minutes depending on the size of the directory you specified.

To Edit Directory Security for a Group in Windows Explorer

1. From your Windows NT workstation, launch Windows Explorer by following this sequence:

   Start ➢ Programs ➢ Windows Explorer

2. Browse through the file system until you find the C:\TEMP directory.
3. At the top of the screen, click the Security option and select Permissions from the drop-down menu.
4. In the Name window of the Permissions screen, highlight the Everyone group.
5. Click the Type Of Access drop-down menu and select Read.
6. Above the Name window, select the "Replace permissions on subdirectories" and "Replace permissions on existing files" check boxes.
7. In the lower-left corner, click OK. The system will replace directory rights to the C:\TEMP directory.
8. In the upper-right corner of the window, click the X button to close Windows Explorer.

LAB 21: LAB REPORT

DATE ____________________ NAME ____

1. What is the importance of controlling security on the network?

____

____

____

____

2. Why is it preferable to grant rights through groups rather than through individual users?

____

____

____

____

3. In Windows NT, what utility do you use to edit file system security?

____

____

____

____

4. In Windows NT, what types of access to the file system can you grant with permissions?

____

____

____

____

Lab 22: Add and Change Security Rights in a NetWare 5 Network

Objectives

Upon completion of this lab, you will be able to:

1. Add security rights to an NDS object using NetWare Administrator.
2. Change security rights to an NDS object using NetWare Administrator.

Suggested Reading

Chapter 8, pages 319–334, *Network+ Study Guide*, David Groth, Sybex.

Hardware Needed

An operational Windows 95 workstation attached to a NetWare 5 network.

Software Needed

NetWare Administrator.

Introduction

As a network administrator, you must understand how to control users' access to the resources available on the network. In a NetWare 5 environment, the utility used to control the security of both the file system and the NDS tree is NetWare Administrator.

In this lab, you will learn the tools available in NetWare Administrator to control the network's security.

PROCEDURE

To Add Security Rights to a User in NetWare Administrator

1. From your Windows 95 workstation, launch NetWare Administrator. This utility is in the SYS:\PUBLIC\WIN32 directory on the NetWare 5 Server.
2. Browse the NDS tree to find a user object. Right-click the USER object. (Write down the username. You will need this information later.)
3. From the menu that appears, choose Details. The Details window opens.
4. From the menu on the right side of the window, click the Group Membership option. Write down any groups that this user belongs to.
5. At the bottom of the window, click the Cancel button.
6. Browse the NDS tree for a container object. Right-click a container object. From the menu that appears, choose Trustees Of This Object.

> **NOTE** To open the trustee list, you can also click and drag the USER object onto the container object.

7. The trustee list appears. If the USER object that you are using is a member of any of the groups listed here, delete the trustee assignment by highlighting that group in the list and choosing Delete Trustee.
8. Click the Add Trustee button, which is to the right of the trustee list. Browse the tree to find the user object you found in step 2. Click OK.
9. To give this user supervisory rights to the container, select the Supervisor check box.
10. To close the window, click OK.

To Change Security Rights to an Object in NDS

1. Browse the NDS tree to find a container object. Right-click a container object. From the menu that appears, select Trustees Of This Object.
2. In the trustee list, find a trustee assignment. Click the NDS object listed in the trustee list to see the rights this object is assigned at the container.
3. To give this object Supervisor rights to the NDS container, select the Supervisor check box.
4. To close the window, click OK.

To Verify the Assigned Rights in NDS

1. Find an NDS object beneath the container you changed assigned rights to in the second exercise of this lab.
2. Right-click the object. From the menu that appears, choose Trustees Of This Object.
3. Click the Effective Rights button.
4. Click the Search button, which is to the right of the Object Name check box. Browse the tree for the object whose rights you changed in the second exercise of this lab. To select the object, double-click it.
5. Write down the object rights listed in this screen. This user should have the Supervisor right.
6. At the bottom of the window, click Close.

LAB 22: LAB REPORT

DATE ____________________ NAME ____

1. Why is understanding how to manage security on your network important?

____

____

____

____

2. List two ways to make a user a trustee of a container object.

____

____

____

____

3. What are effective rights?

____

____

____

____

4. How can you delete a trustee assignment?

____

____

____

____

Lab 23: Implement a Full Backup with the SBackup Utility

Objectives

Upon completion of this lab, you will be able to:

1. Prepare the NetWare 5 Server for a backup.
2. Complete the backup using the NetWare SBackup utility.

Suggested Reading

Chapter 10, pages 429–441, *Network+ Study Guide*, David Groth, Sybex.

Hardware Needed

1. A functional NetWare 5 Server.
2. A backup device attached to this server.

Software Needed

None.

Introduction

It is imperative to back up network data in order to prevent data loss. This protection of network data is an important and necessary procedure on every network. There are various types of backup procedures. The backup procedure used should be appropriate for your particular network.

In addition to performing the backup on your system, you should maintain a log of the backups you have completed. You can record any errors that have occurred, the length of time it took to back up your data, and any other pertinent information. Another important safety measure is to store backup tapes offsite. For example, you can keep the tapes in a safety deposit box at the bank or in a fireproof safe in some other location. This will protect the data on the system even if a disaster occurs onsite.

In this lab, you will complete a *full backup*. This will back up all data on the network in its entirety. With a full backup, you can quickly restore the network data when the need arises. Other backup strategies, such as *incremental* or *differential* procedures, systematically back up data. These backup procedures require less time to complete than a full backup, but they also require more time to recover the network data when the need arises.

There are also several utilities available to back up network data. In this lab, you will use the SBackup utility, which comes with the NetWare 5 software package.

PROCEDURE

To Prepare for the Backup

1. Verify that the tape device is attached and configured to the NetWare 5 Server.
2. Go to the server console. At the server console, type the command to load the following NLMs (NetWare Loadable Modules):

   TSANDS

   TSASMS

3. The system will load the support modules automatically. Watch the scrolling information to verify the process.

To Complete the Backup

1. To load the SBackup utility at the server console, type the following:

   sbackup

2. The system will request a **target** (a system to be backed up). Request NDS backup by selecting NDS.
3. The Login Request screen appears. Log in as the Admin user. Verify that you are using a login that has Supervisor rights at the root of the NDS tree.
4. SBackup will allow you to choose the device to back up the NDS information to. There should be only one device to choose from. To select this device, press Enter.
5. Select the root of the SYS: volume to create and save the error and log file. The files are copied to this location.
6. The Backup Type screen appears. Select the Full option to back up all NDS information to the tape backup device.
7. The system requests a description of the backup session. Enter the date in numerical format.
8. The screen prompts you to back up now, later, or to cancel the backup procedure. Scroll down to the Backup Now option and press Enter.
9. Put the tape into the backup device.
10. Enter a label for the media. For this lab, enter the present date in numerical form.
11. Press the Proceed With Backup option. The backup begins. All of the NDS information will be backed up to the tape.
12. You may require more than one tape. Insert the tapes as requested.
13. When the backup is complete, remove the tape from the tape backup device.

LAB 23: LAB REPORT

DATE ____________________ NAME ______________________________________

1. Why is a good backup schedule a necessity in any network?

2. List the three types of backup procedures available.

3. Which type of backup did you perform on the NetWare 5 Server?

4. What NLMs are required to prepare for a backup using the SBackup utility?

Lab 24: Install and Run an Anti-Virus Software Program

Objectives

Upon completion of this lab, you will be able to:

1. Find an anti-virus software program on the Internet.
2. Download the anti-virus program from the Internet.
3. Install and run the anti-virus program on your workstation.

Suggested Reading

Chapter 10, pages 441–446, *Network+ Study Guide*, David Groth, Sybex.

Hardware Needed

A functional Windows 95 workstation with Internet connectivity.

Software Needed

1. An anti-virus software program, which you will download from the Internet.
2. A Web browser installed on the workstation.

Introduction

A computer program that copies itself to other programs and infects them is a computer *virus*. The virus is activated when a computer user runs an infected program. Simply opening a text document or reading an e-mail message can activate a virus.

The simplest way to avoid infection is not to install or open anything on your computer. Of course, this is not an option. Therefore, you need to be careful about what you do install and what you do open. You can also establish good virus-protection guidelines and procedures, such as the following:

- Only open files that come from reliable sources.
- Run an anti-virus software program.

When you install an anti-virus software package, it will check your computer for viruses. The anti-virus software must be updated as new updates are available. New viruses are coming out every day, and the integrity of your data relies on the abilities of your anti-virus program to recognize and remove viruses from your system.

In this lab, you will download an anti-virus program from the Internet. You will also install and run the program on your computer.

PROCEDURE

To Download an Anti-Virus Software Package from the Internet

1. Launch your Web browser.
2. In the address field, enter **www.antivirus.com**. You will be connected to Trend Micro, Incorporated home page.

> **NOTE** Trend Micro, Inc. offers a free 30-day trial version of their anti-virus software, PC-cillin6. There are several other good anti-virus programs available.

3. Click the Download Free 30 Day Trial option.
4. The Form screen will appear. Fill in the required personal information and click Submit.
5. In the next window, find the appropriate platform version, which is Windows 95 and Windows 98. Click Download PC-cillin 6.
6. To save the file, specify the desired location on the C: drive and click Download.
7. The file will download. When it is complete, close the Browser window.

To Install the Anti-Virus Software

1. Open My Computer. Find the PCC6(1).EXE file.
2. Double-click this file to launch the executable. You will get the message "This will install Trend PC-cillin. Do you wish to continue?" Click Yes.
3. The initial Installation screen appears. Click Next.
4. The License Agreement screen launches. To accept the agreement, click Yes. The installation will continue by scanning the system for existing viruses. If you do not have existing viruses, click OK on the Information screen.
5. A window asking for the name, company, and serial number will appear. Leave the Serial Number field blank. Click Next.
6. Without the serial number, the 30-day trial version appears. To install the software, click Next.
7. The installation continues with the Program Folder specification. Click Next.
8. Click Next in the following two windows to accept the default installation parameters.
9. The files will be installed. At this time, you can choose to create an emergency boot disk. You will need three formatted floppies to create the boot disk. For this exercise, choose Skip.
10. Click Finish to complete the installation.

To Request a Scan of a Drive

1. To find the software program, look in your System Tray. To launch PC-cillin to scan your system, right-click and choose Open.
2. Select the drive you want scanned. In the upper-right corner of the window, click the Scan icon.
3. The software will scan the chosen drive for any viruses. This may take a few minutes.
4. In the Results window, click OK. If the software located a virus on your system, the Results window will display the name of the virus that was found and whether or not the virus was successfully removed from your system (see Figure 24.1).

FIGURE 24.1 Results window

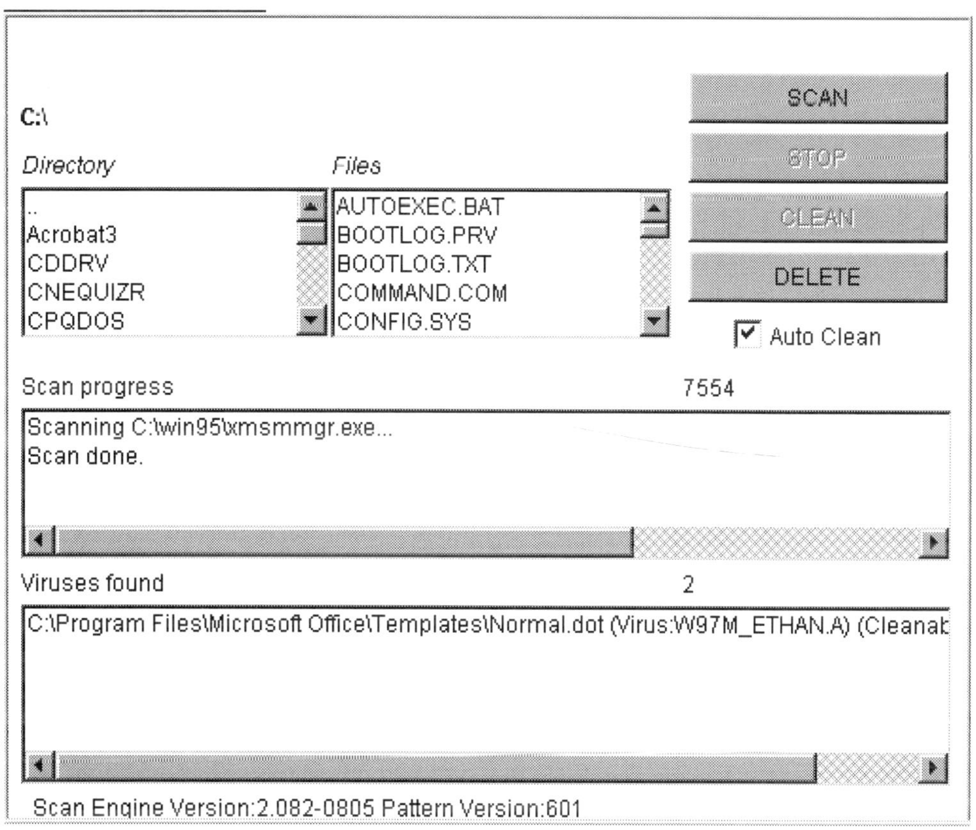

LAB 24: LAB REPORT

DATE ____________________ NAME ____

1. What is a computer virus?

____

____

____

____

2. What is the purpose of using an anti-virus software program on your workstation?

____

____

____

____

3. Why is it important to update anti-virus software as updates become available?

____

____

____

____

4. On what Windows Desktop utility does the anti-virus program reside?

____

____

____

____

Lab 25: Use Novell's Web Site to Solve a Technical Problem

Objectives

Upon completion of this lab, you will be able to:

1. Use Novell's Technical Support Web site to find answers to technical issues.

Suggested Reading

Chapter 11, *Network+ Study Guide*, David Groth, Sybex.

Hardware Needed

An operational Windows 95 workstation with an active Internet connection.

Software Needed

A Web browser installed on the workstation.

Introduction

With the touch of the mouse, the Internet allows us to access information that would have taken hours or days to find five years ago. With the Internet's valuable resources, we can connect to administrators around the globe and get solutions from the most respected and informed engineers available. Because of its power to link us to information, administrators must understand how to use the Internet's resources.

This lab will introduce you to Novell's Technical Support Web site and the tools available there. In this lab, you will use Novell's site to do two things:

- Find the most recent client software for your Windows 95 workstation.
- Find information on how to solve the problem of a server **ABEND** (the Novell term referring to a malfunction on the server) in TSANDS.NLM when backing up NDS.

PROCEDURE

To Find the Most Recent Client Software for a Windows 95 Workstation

1. Launch a Web browser program.
2. At the address line, enter **support.novell.com**. This will take you to Novell's Technical Support Web site.
3. Browse the page and become familiar with the layout of the Technical Support page.
4. To find the client software download, find the Product Specific Information drop-down box on Novell's home page.
5. Click the down arrow to display the available products. Scroll down to find the NetWare Client v3.1 for Windows 95/98. Click this option.
6. The Client Information screen appears. Here you can find **TIDs** (Technical Information Documents) with information on client software problems.
7. From the top of the screen, click File Finder.
8. From the File Finder window, click the Download Novell Clients option. A list of available clients appears.
9. From the list of available clients, click the Clients-Network option.
10. The list of available network clients for NetWare appears. Select the Client v3.1 For Windows 95/98 English option.
11. Below the client specification information, click the Proceed To Download button.
12. Enter the name, country, and e-mail address. This information is required to complete the download. Click Connect.
13. An export restriction notice appears. To accept the export restriction notice, click Accept.
14. The Download screen appears. Click the Inside U.S. button.
15. Click Save It To Disk. Select the floppy or a location on your local machine to download the software.
16. After the download is complete, go back to the home page at `support.novell.com`.

To Find Information on a Server ABEND in TSANDS.NLM when Backing Up NDS

1. If you are not already there, go to the support page of Novell's Web site.
2. At the top of the screen, click the Knowledgebase option. This will bring you to Novell's Knowledgebase window.
3. From the product category list, choose NetWare. To find technical information, select the TIDs option from the Document Set drop-down box.
4. In the Word And Phrase field, enter keywords that will help you find the TID on a server ABEND. For example, type "**ABEND in TSANDS.NLM**" or "**ABEND during backup.**"
5. Click Search Now. Search the TIDs that the system finds. Locate the information needed to resolve the technical issue.

LAB 25: LAB REPORT

DATE ____________________ NAME ____

1. Where can you find the most up-to-date information about technical issues?

____

____

____

____

2. Why is it important to understand how to use a vendor's support site?

____

____

____

3. What information is required to complete the client software download specific to your operating system?

____

____

____

____

4. What type of information did you find when searching for the server ABEND information?

____

____

____

____

Lab 26: Use Microsoft's Web Site to Resolve a Technical Issue

Objectives

Upon completion of this lab, you will be able to:

1. Use Microsoft's Technical Support Web site to resolve technical problems.

Suggested Reading

Chapter 11, pages 509–510, *Network+ Study Guide*, David Groth, Sybex.

Hardware Needed

A functional Windows 95 workstation with an active Internet connection.

Software Needed

A Web browser installed in the workstation.

Introduction

The single ability that makes a good network administrator is the ability to solve network problems. If you cannot resolve the issues encountered in your network, you are not doing your job. Of course, it is impossible for a single person to know all the answers. Therefore, it is very important to know where to find the answers. If you become familiar with the tools available, it is much simpler to solve problems as they arise.

In this lab, you will be introduced to tools to find the answers to two problems:

- How to install the Windows 95 service pack
- How to fix a 266 error on a SQL Server

PROCEDURE

To Find Out How to Install the Windows 95 Service Pack

1. Open the Web browser on your workstation.
2. In the location field, enter the URL to Microsoft's Technical Support Web site:

   http://support.microsoft.com

3. The Knowledge Base Search page launches. In the My Search Is About field, click the down arrow to find Windows 95. Select the Windows 95 option.
4. In the I Want To Search By field, select the Keywords radio button.
5. In the My Question Is field, enter **Service Pack.**
6. In the Search Options area, choose the Full Text radio button.
7. In the I Want The Search Results To Show field, select the Titles With Excerpts radio button.
8. Click Go. The search will find information on Microsoft's site that matches the requested parameters.
9. Search the Results window for the article "How to: Install the Windows 95 Service Pack 1 Upgrade."

To Find Out about Error 266 on a SQL Server

1. Launch the Web browser on the workstation.
2. In the location line, enter the address to Microsoft's support site:

   http://support.microsoft.com

3. In the My Search Is About field, enter **SQL Server** (see Figure 26.1).
4. In the I Want To Search By field, select the Keywords radio button.
5. In the My Question Is field, enter **Error 266.**
6. Choose the Full Text search option.
7. In the I Want The Search Results To Show field, choose the Title With Excerpts search parameter.
8. Click Go to begin the search.
9. Find the article "Q158325 – INF: Stored Procedures, Transactions, and Error 266." Review the information to resolve the error.

FIGURE 26.1 Searching the Microsoft Technical Support Web Site

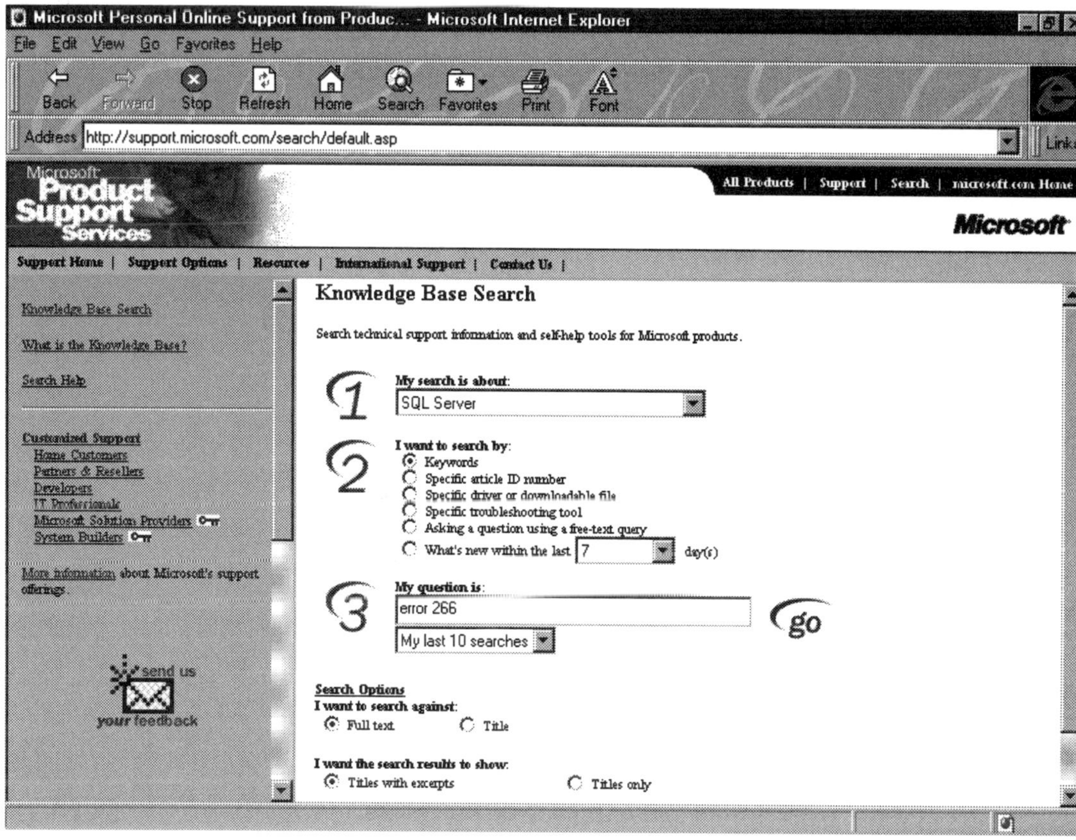

10. At the top of the screen, click Support Options.
11. On the support page, select Product To Find.
12. Click the down arrow and select the SQL Server option.
13. To start the search, click Go. The search results will provide you with more resources to research the problem you encountered. The resources include Web sites, phone numbers, and articles.
14. Close the Web Browser window.

LAB 26: LAB REPORT

DATE ____________________ NAME ____

1. List three reasons why you would use a vendor's Technical Support Web site.

2. What is the URL to Microsoft's Technical Support Web site?

3. What is Microsoft's information database called?

4. Where can you find additional troubleshooting resources on Microsoft's Technical Support Web site?

Lab 27: Use the Monitor Utility in a NetWare 5 Network to Analyze Network Performance

Objectives

Upon completion of this lab, you will be able to:

1. Understand the critical information provided by the Monitor utility.
2. Determine possible problem areas in the network based on information provided by the Monitor utility.
3. Understand the network connection information provided by the Monitor utility.

Suggested Reading

Chapter 11, page 514, *Network+ Study Guide*, David Groth, Sybex.

Hardware Needed

A functional NetWare 5 Server.

Software Needed

None.

Introduction

There are several utilities that allow you to determine the baseline usage of a network. A *baseline* is defined as the average network readings during normal use of network resources. To determine if there is a problem on your network, you can compare the current readings with the baseline reading statistics.

A network administrator can compare current readings to baseline readings with the Monitor utility. Understanding the information provided by the Monitor utility allows the administrator to pinpoint, or at least make an educated guess about, the source of the problem.

In this lab, you will examine the baseline readings of a network. You will compare this information to current readings. Based on given information, you will determine the issues that are causing the network's inefficiency.

PROCEDURE

To Determine a Network's Baseline Reading

1. To load the Monitor utility, type the following at the server console:

    MONITOR

2. The General Information screen appears. Write down the general information. Find the current processor usage provided in the Utilization line (see Figure 27.1). This is the second line in the screen.

FIGURE 27.1 The General Information screen of the Monitor utility

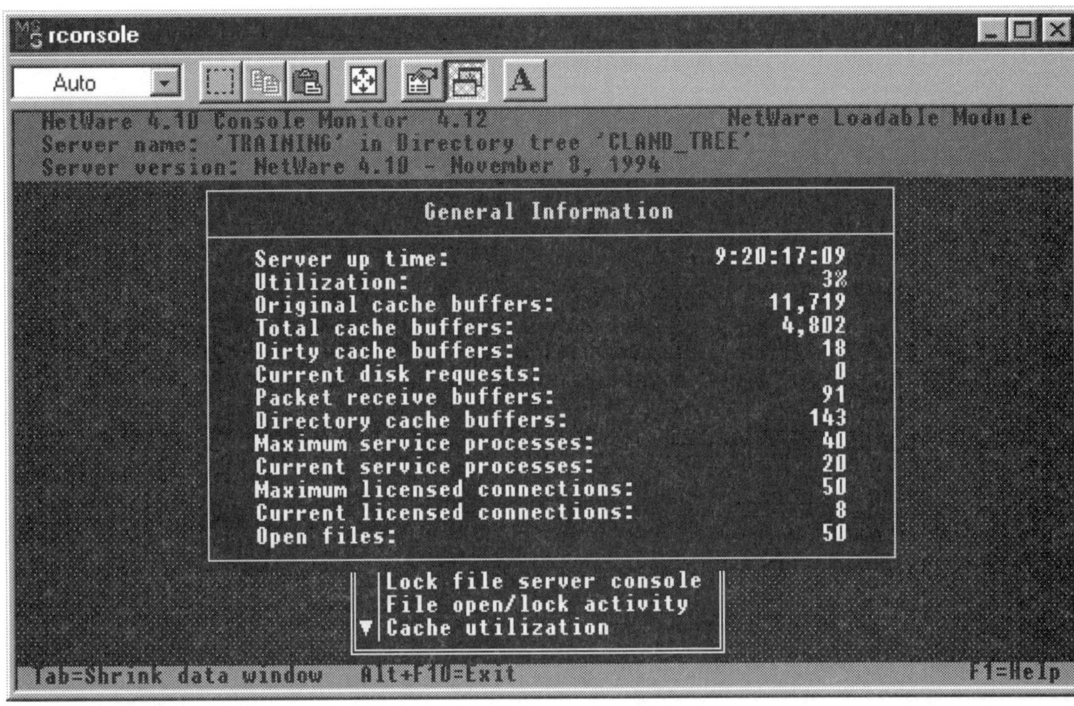

3. The first field in the utility is the Server Up Time. This tells you when the server was last rebooted. Write down this information.

4. Write down the statistics for the cache buffers (lines 3, 4, 5, 7, and 8 in the General Information screen).

TIP When comparing the baseline reading to the current reading, you should be concerned if there is a dramatic rise in the cache buffer numbers.

5. Hit the Tab key. From the lower window, select the Cache Utilization option. Press Enter. The Cache Utilization Statistics screen appears (see Figure 27.2).

FIGURE 27.2 The Cache Utilization Statistics screen of the Monitor utility

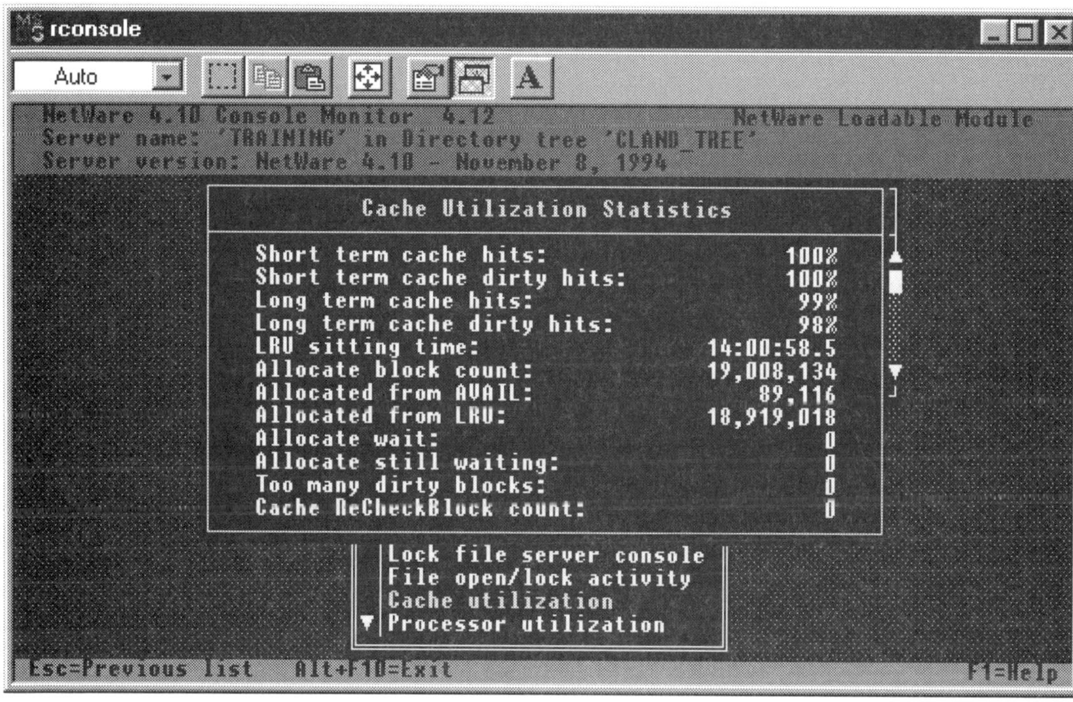

6. Write down the number of cache hits (lines 1–4 of the Cache Utilization Statistics screen).

NOTE If the number of cache hits goes below 90%, the server needs more RAM.

To Increase the Processor Usage on the NetWare Server

1. At the server console, exit Monitor. Hit Escape and answer Yes to exit the utility.

2. At the server console, press Alt+Esc. To increase usage, you will add NLMs to the server.

3. At the server console, enter the following:

   REMOTE [*ENTER A PASSWORD*]

   RSPX

   INSTALL

   FILER

To Check Network Readings after Increasing Usage

1. At the server console, type the following:

   MONITOR

2. Compare the current Monitor statistics to the readings found in the first exercise of this lab.

LAB 27: LAB REPORT

DATE ____________________ NAME ____

1. What is a baseline reading?

____

____

____

____

2. What does the reading from the Utilization line represent?

____

____

____

____

3. If the number of cache hits was 65%, what would you need to do to increase the number?

____

____

____

____

4. List five differences between the first reading and the second reading.

____

____

____

____

Lab 28: Analyze NetWare Volume Statistics

Objectives

Upon completion of this lab, you will be able to:

1. View and analyze network statistics using NetWare Administrator.
2. View and analyze network statistics using Network Neighborhood.

Suggested Reading

Chapter 3, pages 92–94, and Chapter 8, pages 319–321, *Network+ Study Guide*, David Groth, Sybex.

Hardware Needed

A functional Windows 95 workstation attached to a NetWare 5 network.

Software Needed

1. NetWare Administrator.
2. Client32 software installed.

Introduction

In a NetWare network, it is essential to understand volume statistics. This information helps you determine when to perform many vital network maintenance tasks, such as the following:

- When to replace or upgrade hardware
- When to run diagnostic utilities
- When to clean up the file system to create more usable volume space
- When to make your volume space usage more efficient

In this lab, you will examine two utilities that allow you to determine volume space usage: NetWare Administrator and Network Neighborhood.

PROCEDURE

To View Volume Statistics with Network Neighborhood

1. Turn on the Windows 95 workstation. The computer will boot to the Windows 95 Desktop.
2. When prompted at the Client32 Login screen, log into the NetWare 5 Server using an administrator password.
3. On the Desktop, double-click Network Neighborhood.
4. Double-click the NetWare 5 Server to display the available volumes.
5. Click once on the SYS: volume to highlight it.
6. Right-click the SYS: volume. From the menu that appears, select Properties.
7. At the top of the window, click the NetWare Volume Statistics tab. Analyze the graph and write down the information (see Figure 28.1).

FIGURE 28.1 The NetWare Volume Statistics tab of the Network Neighborhood utility

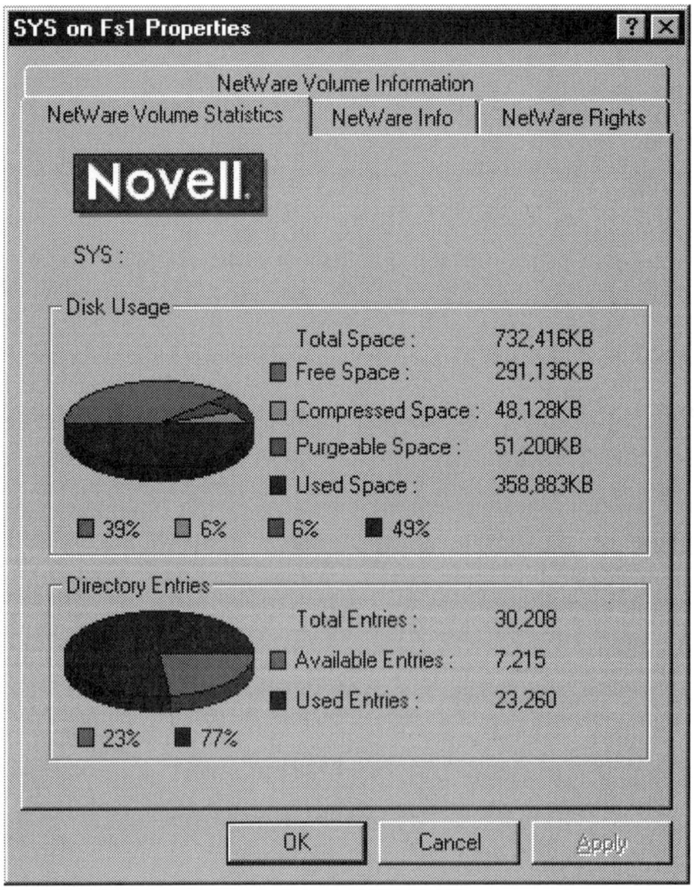

To Analyze Volume Statistics with NetWare Administrator

1. On the workstation, locate NetWare Administrator, found in the following location:

   [*Servername*]_SYS:PUBLIC\WIN32\NWADM32

2. Browse through NetWare Administrator to find the object associated with the SYS: volume.
3. Right-click the NDS object. From the menu that appears, select Details.
4. On the right side of the window, click the Statistics tab (see Figure 28.2). This tab gives you statistics on volume usage, as well as a listing of the installed components. Analyze this information.

FIGURE 28.2 The Statistics tab of the NetWare Administrator utility

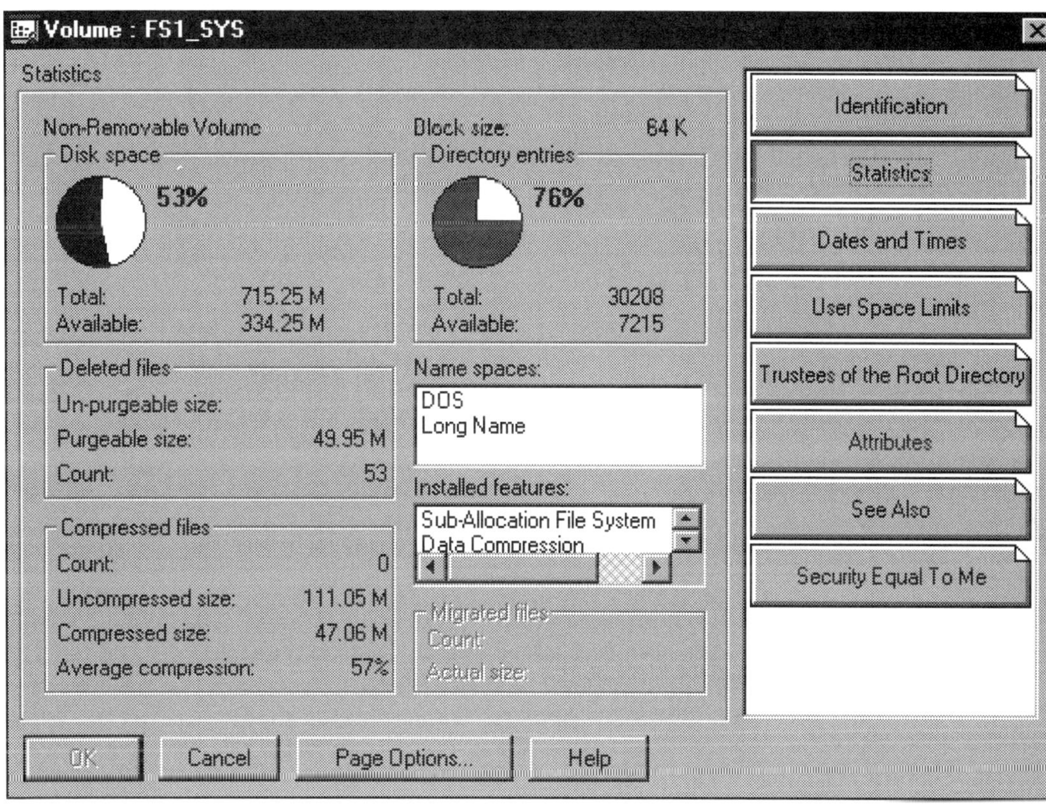

LAB 28: LAB REPORT

DATE ____________________ NAME ____

1. What is the importance of tracking volume usage?

2. List two utilities available to find volume statistics in a NetWare 5 environment.

3. What version of the client allows you to use the features in this lab?

4. What features are installed on your server? Where did you find this information?

Lab 29: Troubleshoot Connectivity Issues on a Multiplatform Network

Objectives

Upon completion of this lab, you will be able to:

1. Troubleshoot connectivity problems on a NetWare 5 Server.
2. Troubleshoot connectivity problems on a Microsoft Windows NT Server.
3. Learn the basic network troubleshooting steps, regardless of the operating system platform.

Suggested Reading

Chapter 11, *Network+ Study Guide*, David Groth, Sybex.

Hardware Needed

1. A NetWare 5 Server.
2. A Microsoft Windows NT Server.
3. A Windows 95 workstation.

Software Needed

None.

Introduction

Today, most networks are comprised of many different operating systems, as well as different cabling types and protocols. As a network administrator, you need to be able to troubleshoot issues that arise on your networks, from the simplest to the most complex. Because the fundamental reason for networks is to share resources and information, a main focus of network administrators is troubleshooting connectivity issues that impede the flow of information in a network.

In this lab, you will practice some of the basic troubleshooting steps necessary to solve connectivity issues. Some steps are vendor-specific; others are useful regardless of the platform your system is running on. First, you will focus on hardware and non-vendor–specific issues. Then, you will troubleshoot specific operating system issues.

PROCEDURE

To Check the Most Common Connectivity Issues When Using TCP/IP

1. Determine if the workstation is cabled properly. Position the workstation so you can see the back panel. Verify that the cable is connected to the NIC. Follow the cable to the hub or wall panel. Verify that the cable is secure in the port.
2. Determine if the workstation sees the NIC. Follow this sequence:

   Start ➢ Programs ➢ MS-DOS prompt

3. Type the following:

   ping 127.0.0.1

4. Verify that you received a positive reply message.
5. To verify that the workstation can see the server, type the following at the MS-DOS prompt:

   ping [*server IP address*]

6. Verify that the workstation has an IP address assigned. At the MS-DOS prompt, type the following:

   winipcfg

7. This will display the IP configuration of the workstation. Verify that there is an IP address and that the gateway is correct.
8. If you need to edit, go to the Control Panel and select the Network tab. Click the Properties button to see the TCP/IP protocol (see Figure 29.1).
9. Find out if any other workstations in the network are having connectivity issues. If they are, the problem is a network issue. If no other workstations are having problems, focus on the specific workstation with problems and its configuration.
10. Try rebooting the workstation.

> **TIP** Rebooting a computer can solve many problems. Before looking at more complex answers, try this simple step.

To Troubleshoot when You Are Unable to Connect to a NetWare 5 Server

1. After rebooting the computer, does the client Login screen appear? If so, you have a connection to the network. If not, the problem lies at the cable or card in the computer.
2. Identify the version of the NetWare client software. To connect to a NetWare 5 Server, you must have software that is version 2.2 or higher.
3. In the Login screen, click the Advanced button. Check the information in the Context text box (see Figure 29.2). Correct this information if the context is invalid or incorrect.

FIGURE 29.1 The Properties button of the Network tab shows the TCP/IP settings that are bound to the board.

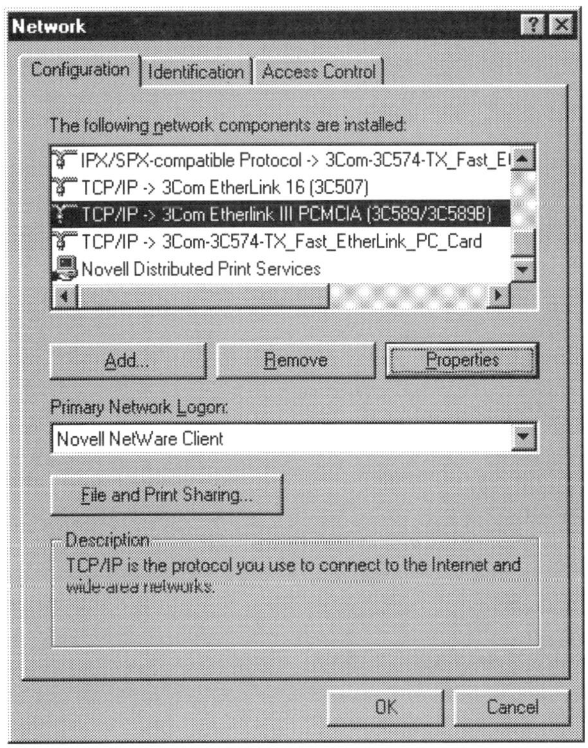

FIGURE 29.2 Checking the Context text box

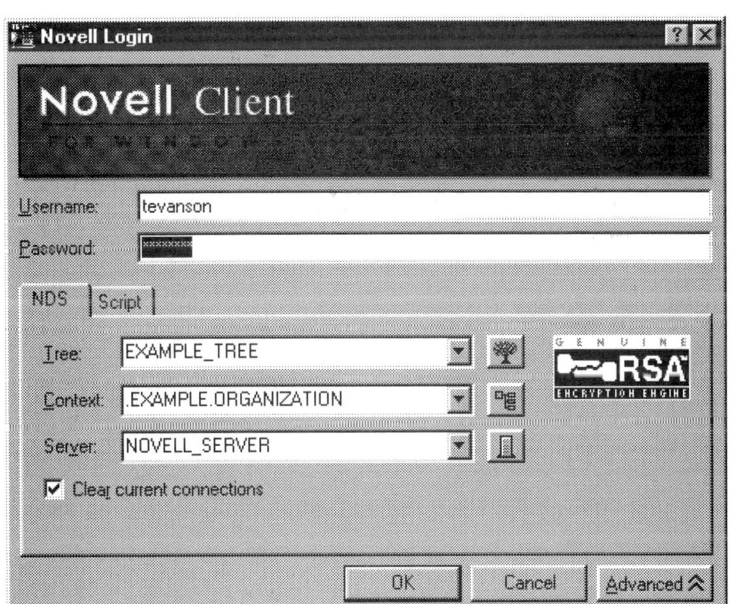

4. Verify the username and password. NetWare is not case sensitive, so you will not have to check for this.
5. Verify that the NetWare 5 server is running. At the server console, verify that you can type characters. Also, verify that you can Alt+Esc through the various programs that are loaded.
6. On your NetWare 5 server, Alt+Esc to the StartX window. From the Novell button in the lower-right corner, select ConsoleOne. Browse through the tree and find your user object. Reset the password.
7. Go back to the workstation. Attempt to log in using the new password.

To Solve Basic Connectivity Issues on a Windows NT Server

1. Verify that the NT Server is running. At the server, see if you can you navigate the window. Make sure the server is not locked up or overworked.
2. Check to make sure that the network cable from the server is intact. Check the back panel of the server. Verify that the cable is tightly inserted.
3. On the back panel, check for the connection light on the NIC port. You will see a light if there is an active network connection.
4. Go back to the workstation. Determine if you have the correct client installed and active on your workstation by following this sequence:

   Start ➢ Settings ➢ Control Panel ➢ Network

5. Verify that the Primary Network Login is set to Client For Microsoft Networks (see Figure 29.3).
6. Verify that you are logging into the correct domain. In the Installed window, highlight Client For Microsoft Networks. Click the Properties button. In the General tab, verify that the domain name is correct (see Figure 29.4).
7. Verify that you are using the correct username and password. Microsoft NT network passwords are case sensitive, so you may need to adjust Caps Lock on the keyboard.

FIGURE 29.3 Selecting the Client for Microsoft Networks option

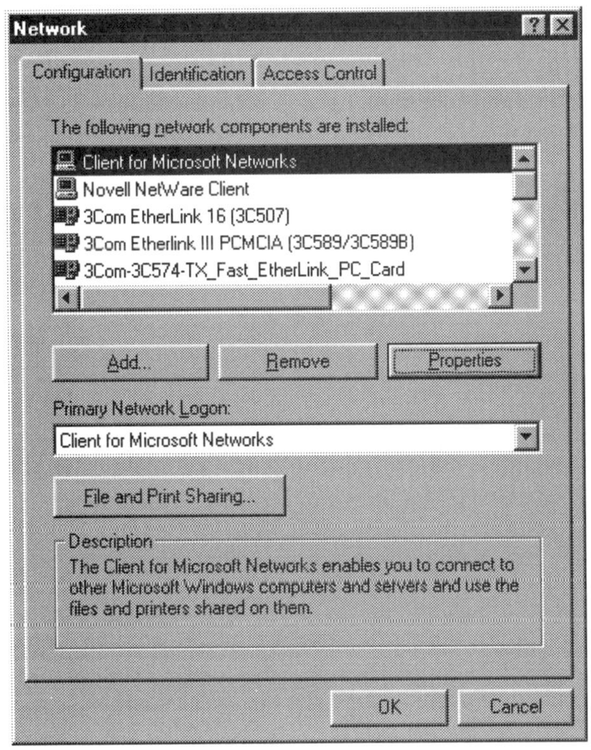

FIGURE 29.4 Checking the domain name

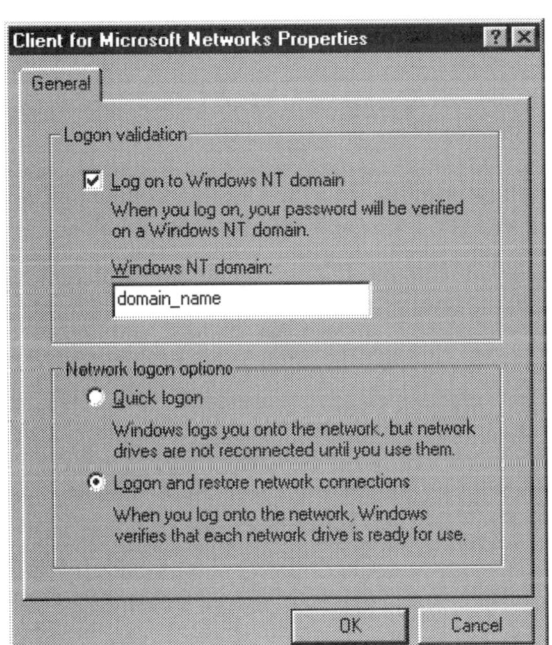

LAB 29: LAB REPORT

DATE ____________________ NAME ______________________________

1. List three basic troubleshooting steps that are not vendor specific.

2. What IP address can you ping to test your NIC?

3. If the NIC is functioning properly and has an active network connection, what physical indicator will you see?

4. List two vendor-specific troubleshooting steps you can use to troubleshoot the inability to log into a NetWare network.

Lab 30: Editing File System Rights in a Linux Environment

Objectives

Upon completion of this lab, you will be able to:

1. Check the permissions to a file in a Linux system.
2. Change the ownership of a file in a Linux system.

Suggested Reading

Chapter 9, *Network+ Study Guide*, David Groth, Sybex.

Hardware Needed

A functional computer with the Linux operating system installed.

Software Needed

None.

Introduction

It is important to secure the file system on your network to avoid unauthorized access to information or damage to the integrity of the data housed there. Although Linux is often considered more secure than many other operating systems, there is quite a bit of controversy surrounding this claim. Some believe that the Linux operating system is less secure because of its open code. Supporters of Linux argue that the administrator of the system has full control and can rewrite code to customize the system, thus allowing for greater security.

There are things you can do to greatly increase the security of the Linux system. Due to the popularity of Linux, much information on securing the network is available to the user. Therefore, you should avoid giving out shell accounts to users unless it is absolutely necessary. A shell account gives the user Administrator access to the file system. This is the most privileged account on the system.

In this lab, you will work with the *chown* and *chmod* utilities. These utilities allow you to change the ownership of files. Chmod is the most commonly used utility for modifying permissions. It allows you to modify the permissions on a file or directory. It is one of the most difficult utilities for new administrators to understand because its format is not standard. The chmod utility breaks down nine fields into three numbers: one to represent owner rights, one to represent group rights, and one to represent world rights. Each number defines three fields (readable, writable, and executable) as follows:

- If a file is readable, it gets four points.
- If a file is writable, it gets two points.
- If a file is executable, it gets one point.

The total number of points will define the file's access privileges. Those with access privileges to the file can read, edit, and modify the file's information.

To perform the procedures in this lab, you must be logged in with a shell account.

PROCEDURES

To Check a User's Permissions on a File

1. Turn on the computer. Let the system boot to the command prompt.
2. At the prompt, type the following:

   int access [*pathname*]

3. Press Enter.
4. The system will return the user's permissions for the file specified by the path. Write down the results.

NOTE Common rights you will see specified are R_OK, W_OK, and X_OK. These specify the ability to read, write to, or test for the existence of a file.

To Change Ownership of a File Using the chown Utility

1. Go to the command prompt.
2. At the command prompt, type the following:

   chown [*newuser filename*]

3. This simple command will change the ownership of the file to the new user. Verify this by following the steps in the first exercise in this lab.

To Modify Permissions of a File Using the chmod Utility

1. Locate the Command screen on your Linux computer.
2. Type the following command at the prompt:

   chmod 444 [*filename*]

   Use the file modified in the second exercise of this lab.

NOTE You modified the security access of 4, signifying read-only status for the owner, the group, and the world.

3. You can follow the same syntax to modify rights to any file in the file system, providing you are using the correct account for modification (shell account). Note this table when assigning rights.

Number Assignment	Permissions Granted
0	None
1	Execute only
2	Write and Execute only
3	Write and Execute only (rarely used)
4	Read only
5	Read and Execute, but not Write
6	Read and Write, but not Execute
7	Read, Write, Execute

LAB 30: LAB REPORT

DATE ____________________ NAME ____

1. List two ways to secure the file system.

2. What is the most privileged account on a Linux machine?

3. What command allows you to find the file system rights for a user?

4. For the chmod command, list three rights and their meaning.

Glossary of Networking Terms

10Base2 Ethernet An implementation of Ethernet that specifies a 10Mbps signaling rate, baseband signaling, and coaxial cable with a maximum segment length of 185 meters (*xxx* feet).

ABEND Short for ABnormal END. Novell's term for a server crash.

active monitor Used in Token Ring networks, a process that prevents data frames from roaming the ring unchecked. If the frame passes the active monitor too many times, it is removed from the ring. Also ensures that a token is always circulating in the ring.

anti-virus A category of software that uses various methods to eliminate viruses in a computer. It typically also protects against future infection. *See also* virus.

application server Any server that hosts a network application.

ARP table A table used by the ARP protocol. Contains a list of known TCP/IP addresses and their associated MAC addresses. The table is cached in memory so that ARP lookups do not have to be performed for frequently accessed TCP/IP and MAC addresses. *See also* Transmission Control Protocol/Internet Protocol.

Attachment Unit Interface (AUI) port Port on some NICs that allows connecting the NIC to different media types by using an external transceiver.

bandwidth In network communications, the amount of data that can be sent across a wire in a given time. Each communication that passes along the wire decreases the amount of available bandwidth.

baseband A transmission technique in which the signal uses the entire bandwidth of a transmission medium.

baseline A category of network documentation that indicates how the network normally runs. It includes such information as network statistics, server utilization trends, and processor performance statistics.

Bit Fiddler A virus that changes small random bits in files.

BNC connector Tubular connectors most commonly used with coaxial cable.

boot sector virus A virus that overrides the boot sector, therefore making it appear as if there is no pointer to your operating system. When this happens, you will see a Missing Operating System or Hard Disk Not Found error message on power-up.

broadband A network transmission method in which a single transmission medium is divided so that multiple signals can travel across the same medium simultaneously.

browser A computer program that uses the Hypertext Transfer Protocol and is used on a workstation to access hosts on the Web.

cable A physical transmission medium that has a central conductor of wire or fiber surrounded by a plastic jacket.

cable map A general network documentation indicating each cable's source and destination, as well as where each network cable runs.

Carrier Sense Multiple Access/Collision Avoidance (CSMA/CA) A media access method that sends a Request To Send (RTS) packet and waits to receive a Clear To Send (CTS) packet before sending. Once the CTS is received, the sender sends the packet of information.

Carrier Sense Multiple Access/Collision Detection (CSMA/CD) A media access method that first senses whether there is a signal on the wire, indicating that someone is transmitting currently. If no one else is transmitting, it attempts a transmission and listens to hear whether someone else tries to transmit at the same time. If this happens, both senders back off and don't transmit again until some random period of time has passed.

client/server network A server-centric network in which all resources are stored on a file server. Processing power is distributed among workstations and the file server.

coaxial cable Often referred to as *coax*. A type of cable used in network wiring. Typical coaxial cable types include RG-58 and RG-62. 10Base2 Ethernet networks use coaxial cable. Coaxial cable is usually shielded.

cold site backup system A backup system that does not run continuously. Therefore, before you can restore data, the computer must be repaired, and the software must be reloaded on the server.

crossover cable The troubleshooting tool used in Ethernet UTP installations to test communications between two stations, bypassing the hub. *See also* unshielded twisted-pair.

CSMA/CA *See* Carrier Sense Multiple Access/Collision Avoidance.

CSMA/CD *See* Carrier Sense Multiple Access/Collision Detection.

data packet A unit of data sent over a network. A packet includes a header, addressing information, and the data itself. A packet is treated as a single unit as it is sent from device to device.

default gateway The router that all packets are sent to when the workstation doesn't know where the destination station is or when it can't find the destination station on the local segment.

DHCP *See* Dynamic Host Configuration Protocol.

differential backup Backs up data that has changed since the last full backup.

directory A network database that contains a listing of all network resources, such as users, printers, groups, and so on.

directory services A network service that provides access to a central database of information that contains detailed information about the network resources available on a network.

disk drivers NLMs that provide NetWare with access to the disk channel. *See also* NetWare Loadable Module.

DNS resolver Client software used to make requests of the DNS server in order to resolve DNS host names into IP addresses. *See also* Domain Name Service; Internet Protocol.

DNS server Any server that performs DNS host name to IP address resolution. *See also* Domain Name Service; Internet Protocol.

Domain Name Service (DNS) The network service used in TCP/IP networks that translates host names to IP addresses. *See also* Transmission Control Protocol/Internet Protocol.

drive mapping The process of assigning a drive letter at the client to a directory or folder on the server.

dynamic entry An entry made in the ARP table whenever an ARP request is made by the Windows TCP/IP stack and the MAC address is not found in the ARP table. The ARP request is broadcast on the local segment. When the MAC address of the requested IP address is found, that information is added to the ARP table. *See also* Internet Protocol; Transmission Control Protocol/Internet Protocol.

Dynamic Host Configuration Protocol (DHCP) A protocol used on a TCP/IP-based network to send client configuration data, including TCP/IP address, default gateway, subnet mask, and DNS configuration, to clients. *See also* Domain Name Service; default gateway; subnet mask; Transmission Control Protocol/Internet Protocol.

electromagnetic interference (EMI) The interference that can occur during transmissions over copper cable because of electromagnetic energy outside the cable. The result is degradation of the signal.

electrostatic discharge (ESD) A problem that exists when two items with dissimilar static electrical charges are brought together. The static electrical charges jump to the item with fewer electrical charges, causing ESD that can damage computer components.

emergency scan A scan used after a virus has taken control of a computer. An emergency anti-virus boot disk is used.

EMI *See* electromagnetic interference.

encoding The process of translating data into signals that can be transmitted on a transmission medium.

ESD *See* electrostatic discharge.

Ethernet A shared-media network architecture that operates at the Physical and Data Link layers of the OSI model. It uses baseband signaling over either a bus or a star topology, with CSMA/CD as the media access method. The cabling used in Ethernet networks can be coax, twisted-pair, or fiber-optic. *See also* Carrier Sense Multiple Access/Collision Detection.

fiber-optic A type of network cable that uses a central glass or plastic core surrounded by a plastic coating.

file server A server specialized in holding and distributing files.

File Transfer Protocol (FTP) A TCP/IP protocol and software that permit the transferring of files between computer systems. Because FTP has been implemented on numerous types of computer systems, files can be transferred between disparate computer systems (for example, a personal computer and a minicomputer). *See also* Transmission Control Protocol/Internet Protocol.

FQDN *See* Fully Qualified Domain Name.

FTP *See* File Transfer Protocol.

full backup A backup that copies all the data to the archive medium.

Fully Qualified Domain Name (FQDN) An address that uses both the hostname (workstation name) and the domain name.

gateway The hardware and software needed to connect two disparate network environments so that communications can occur.

global group A type of group in Windows NT that is used network-wide . Members can be from anywhere in the network, and rights can be assigned to any resource in the network.

grouping One way to organize users that eases network administration, such as administrator groups, printer groups, and so on.

Hardware address A Data Link layer address assigned to every NIC at the MAC sublayer. The address is in the format *xx:xx:xx:xx:xx:xx*; each *xx* is a two-digit hexadecimal number. *See also* network interface card.

header The section of a packet where the source and destination address reside.

hop One pass through a router.

host Any network device with a TCP/IP network address. *See also* Transmission Control Protocol/Internet Protocol.

HTTP *See* Hypertext Transfer Protocol.

Hypertext Markup Language (HTML) A set of codes used to format text and graphics that will be displayed in a browser. The codes define how data will be displayed.

Hypertext Transfer Protocol (HTTP) The protocol used for communication between a Web server and a Web browser.

incremental backup Backs up data that has changed since the last full or incremental backup.

Internet A global network made up of a large number of individual networks interconnected through the use of public telephone lines and TCP/IP protocols. *See also* Transmission Control Protocol/Internet Protocol.

Internet Protocol (IP) The protocol in the TCP/IP protocol suite responsible for network addressing and routing. *See also* Transmission Control Protocol/Internet Protocol.

Internet Service Provider (ISP) A company that provides direct access to the Internet for home and business computer users.

Internetwork Packet eXchange (IPX) A connectionless, routable network protocol based on the Xerox XNS architecture. It is the default protocol for versions of NetWare before NetWare 5. It operates at the Network layer of the OSI model and is responsible for addressing and routing packets to workstations or servers on other networks.

IP *See* Internet Protocol.

IP address An address used by the Internet Protocol that identifies the device's location on the network.

IP proxy All communications look as if they originated from a proxy server because the IP address of the user who is making a request is hidden. Also known as network address translation (NAT).

ipconfig A Windows NT utility used to display that machine's current configuration.

IPX *See* Internetwork Packet eXchange.

IPX network address A number that represents an entire network. All servers on the network must use the same external network number.

ISP *See* Internet Service Provider.

Java A programming language, developed by Sun Microsystems, that is used to write programs that will run on any platform that has a Java Virtual Machine installed.

LAN *See* local area network.

LAN driver The interface between the NetWare kernel and the NIC installed in the server. Also a general category of drivers used to enable communications between an operating system and a NIC. *See also* network interface card.

link light A small light-emitting diode (LED) that is found on both the NIC and the hub. It is usually green and labeled Link or something similar. A link light indicates that the NIC and the hub are making a Data Link layer connection. *See also* hub; network interface card.

Linux A version of Unix, developed by Linus Torvalds. Runs on Intel-based PCs and is generally free.

local area network (LAN) A network that is restricted to a single building, group of buildings, or even a single room. A LAN can have one or more servers.

local groups Groups created on individual servers. Rights can be assigned only to local resources.

log file A file that keeps a running list of all errors and notices the time and date they occurred and any other pertinent information.

logical network addressing The addressing scheme used by protocols at the Network layer.

logical bus topology Type of topology in which the signal travels the distance of the cable and is received by all stations on the backbone.

logical ring topology A network topology in which all network signals travel from one station to another, and are read and forwarded by each station.

logical topology Describes the way the information flows. The types of logical topologies are the same as the physical topologies, except that the information flow specifies the type of topology.

MAN *See* metropolitan-area network.

metropolitan-area network (MAN) A network that encompasses an entire city or metropolitan area.

name resolution The process of translating (resolving) logical host names to network addresses

nbtstat (NetBIOS over TCP/IP statistics) The Windows TCP/IP utility that is used to display NetBIOS over TCP/IP statistics. *See also* Transmission Control Protocol/Internet Protocol.

NDS *See* Novell Directory Services.

NDS tree A logical representation of a network's resources. Resources are represented by objects in the tree. The tree is often designed after a company's functional structure. Objects can represent organizations, departments, users, servers, printers, and other resources.

NetBEUI Transport protocol based on the NetBIOS protocol that has datagram support and support for connectionless transmission. *See also* Network Basic Input/Output System.

NetBIOS *See* Network Basic Input/Output System.

netstat A utility used to determine which TCP/IP connections, inbound and outbound, the computer has. It also allows the user to view packet statistics, such as how many have been sent and received. *See also* Transmission Control Protocol/Internet Protocol.

NetWare The network operating system made by Novell.

NetWare 4.*x* The version series of NetWare that includes NDS. *See also* Novell Directory Services.

NetWare 5.*x* The version series of NetWare that includes a multiprocessing kernel. It also includes a five-user version of Oracle 8, a relational database, and the ability to use TCP/IP in its *pure* form.

NetWare Administrator The utility used to administer NetWare versions 4.*x* and later by making changes to the NDS Directory. It is the only administrative utility needed to modify NDS objects and their properties. *See also* Novell Directory Services.

NetWare Loadable Module (NLM) A component used to provide a NetWare server with additional services and functionality. Unneeded services can be unloaded, thus conserving memory.

Network Basic Input/Output System (NetBIOS) A Session layer protocol that opens communication sessions for applications that want to communicate on a network.

network-centric Refers to network operating systems that use directory services that maintain information about the entire network.

network interface card (NIC) Physical device that connects computers and other network equipment to the transmission medium.

network media The physical cables that link computers in a network; also known as physical media.

network operating system (NOS) The software that runs on a network server and offers file, print, application, and other services to clients.

NIC *See* network interface card.

NIC diagnostics Software utilities that verify that the NIC is functioning correctly and that test every aspect of NIC operation. *See also* network interface card.

NIC driver *See* LAN driver.

NLM *See* NetWare Loadable Module.

NOS *See* network operating system.

Novell Directory Services (NDS) A NetWare service that provides access to a global, hierarchical directory database of network entities that can be centrally managed.

Novell Support Connection Novell's database of technical information documents, files, patches, fixes, NetWare Application Notes, Novell lab bulletins, Novell professional developer bulletins, answers to frequently asked questions, and more. The database is available from Novell and is updated quarterly.

NT Directory Services (NTDS) System of domains and trusts for a Windows NT Server network.

NTDS *See* NT Directory Services.

on-access scan An anti-virus scan that is done in the background as a file or a program is opened.

on-demand scan An anti-virus scan that a network administrator or user manually or automatically schedules.

OpenLinux A version of the Linux network operating system developed by Caldera.

packet The basic division of data sent over a network.

patch Software that fixes a problem with an existing program or operating system.

patch cable Any cable that connects one network device to the main cable run or to a patch panel that in turn connects to the main cable run.

patch panel A central wiring point for multiple devices on a UTP network. *See also* unshielded twisted-pair.

peer-to-peer network Computers hooked together that have no centralized authority. Each computer is equal and can act as both a server and a workstation.

physical bus topology A network that uses one network cable that runs from one end of the network to the other. Workstations connect at various points along this cable.

physical media *See* network media.

physical mesh topology A network configuration that specifies a link between each and every device in the network.

physical port An opening on a network device that allows a cable of some kind to be connected. Ports allow devices to be connected to each other with cables.

physical ring topology A network topology that is set up in a circular fashion. Data travels around the ring in one direction, and each device on the ring acts as a repeater to keep the signal strong as it travels. Each device incorporates a receiver for the incoming signal and a transmitter to send the data on to the next device in the ring. The network is dependent on the ability of the signal to travel around the ring.

physical star topology Describes a network in which a cable runs from each network entity to a central device called a hub. The hub allows all devices to communicate as if they were directly connected.

physical topology The physical layout of a network, such as bus, star, ring, or mesh.

Ping A TCP/IP utility used to test whether another host is reachable. An ICMP request is sent to the host who responds with a reply if it is reachable. The request times out if the host is not reachable.

port Some kind of opening that allows network data to pass through. *See* physical port.

POTS Acronym formed from Plain Old Telephone Service. *See* Public Switched Telephone Network.

Plain Old Telephone Service (POTS). Another name for the Public Switched Telephone Network (PSTN). *See* Public Switched Telephone Network.

profile Used in Windows NT to define the user's environment. A user's desktop colors and icons, program groups, Start menu settings, and network connections are remembered in a profile.

protocol A predefined set of rules that dictate how computers or devices communicate and exchange data on the network.

PSTN *See* Public Switched Telephone Network.

Public Switched Telephone Network (PSTN) This is the U.S. public telephone network. It is also called the Plain Old Telephone Service (POTS).

remote access server A computer that has one or more modems installed to enable remote connections to the network.

RG-58 The type designation for the coaxial cable used in thin Ethernet (10Base2). It has a 50-ohm impedance rating and uses BNC connectors.

RG-62 The type designation for the coaxial cable used in ARCNet networks. It has a 93-ohm impedance and uses BNC connectors.

RJ connector A modular connection mechanism that allows for as many as eight copper wires (four pairs). Commonly found in phone (RJ-11) or 10BaseT (RJ-45) connections.

segment A unit of data smaller than a packet. Also a portion of a larger network (a network can consist of multiple network segments).

Sequenced Packet Exchange (SPX) A connection-oriented protocol that is part of the IPX protocol suite. It operates at the Transport layer of the OSI model. It initiates the connection between the sender and the receiver, transmits the data, and then terminates the connection. *See also* Internet Packet eXchange.

server A computer that provides resources to the clients on the network.

server configuration documents General network documentation that includes information such as the current hardware configuration, currently installed software packages, and any installed patches.

Share-level security In a network that uses share-level security, instead of assigning the rights to network resources to users, passwords are assigned to individual files or other network resources (such as printers). These passwords are given to all users that need access to these resources. All resources are visible from anywhere in the network, and any user who knows the password for a particular network resource can make changes to it.

shielded twisted-pair A type of cabling that includes pairs of copper conductors, twisted around each other, inside a metal or foil shield. This type of medium can support faster speeds than nonshielded wiring.

signaling The process of transmitting data across a medium. Two types of signaling are digital and analog.

SPX *See* Sequenced Packet Exchange.

static entry An entry that is added to a Windows ARP table manually.

subnet mask A group of selected bits that identify a subnetwork within a TCP/IP network. *See also* Transmission Control Protocol/Internet Protocol.

subnetwork A network that is part of another network. The connection is made through a gateway, bridge, or router.

TCP *See* Transmission Control Protocol.

TCP/IP *See* Transmission Control Protocol/Internet Protocol.

test account An account set up by an administrator to confirm the basic functionality of a newly installed application, for example. The test account has equal rights to accounts that will use the new functions. It is important to use test accounts instead of administrator accounts to test new functions. If an administrator account is used, problems related to user rights may not manifest themselves because administrator accounts typically have full rights to all network resources.

topology The physical and/or logical layout of the transmission media specified in the physical and logical layers of the OSI model.

tracert The TCP/IP trace route command line utility that shows the user every router interface a TCP/IP packet passes through on its way to a destination. *See also* Transmission Control Protocol/Internet Protocol.

Transmission Control Protocol The protocol found at the Host-to-Host layer of the DOD model. This protocol breaks data packets into segments, numbers them, and sends them in random order. The receiving computer reassembles the data so that the information is readable for the user. In the process, the sender and the receiver confirm that all data has been received; if not, it is resent. This is a connection-oriented protocol.

Transmission Control Protocol/Internet Protocol The protocol suite developed by the DOD in conjunction with the Internet. It was designed as an internetworking protocol suite that could route information around network failures. Today it is the de facto standard for communications on the Internet.

transmission media Physical cables and/or wireless technology across which computers are able to communicate.

twisted-pair cable A type of network transmission medium that contains pairs of color-coded, insulated copper wires that are twisted around each other. A twisted-pair cable consists of one or more twisted pairs in a common jacket.

Uniform Resource Locator (URL) A URL is one way of identifying a document on the Internet. It consists of the protocol that is used to access the document and the domain name or IP address of the host that holds the document; for example, `http://www.sybex.com`.

unshielded twisted-pair cable Twisted-pair cable consisting of a number of twisted pairs of copper wire with a simple plastic casing. Because no shielding is used in this cable, it is very susceptible to EMI, RFI, and other types of interference. *See also* electromagnetic interference.

URL *See* Uniform Resource Locator.

User Manager for Domains The Windows NT utility that you use to manage all users, groups, and policies for a Windows NT domain.

user-level security A type of network in which user accounts can read, write, change, and take ownership of files. Rights are assigned to user accounts. Each user knows only their own username and password, which makes this the preferred method for securing files.

Utility NLM An NLM that is not a LAN driver, disk driver, name space module, or platform support module; for example, MONITOR.NML or INSTALL.NLM. *See also* NetWare Loadable Module.

virus A program intended to damage a computer system. Sophisticated viruses encrypt and hide in a computer and may not appear until the user performs a certain action or until a certain date. *See also* anti-virus.

virus engine The core program that runs the virus-scanning process.

volume A logical way of organizing disk space into usable sections.

WAN *See* wide area network.

wide area network (WAN) A network that crosses local, regional, and international boundaries.

Windows NT A network operating system, developed by Microsoft, that uses the same graphical interface as the Desktop environment, Windows 95.

Windows NT 4 The version of Windows NT based on the look and feel of Windows 95/98. *See also* Windows NT.

winipcfg The IP configuration utility for Windows 95/98 that allows you to view the current TCP/IP configuration of a workstation.

World Wide Web (WWW) A collection of HTTP servers running on the Internet. They support the use of documents formatted with HTML. *See also* HyperText Markup Language; Hypertext Transfer Protocol.

X Window A graphical user interface (GUI) developed for use with the various flavors of Unix.